Collins

Student Support Materials for Edexcel AS History

Unit 1 D4

Stalin's Russia, 1924–53

Series editor: Angela Leonard

Authors: Kerry Killin and Ben Gregory

William Collins' dream of knowledge for all began with the publication of his first book in 1819. A self-educated mill worker, he not only enriched millions of lives, but also founded a flourishing publishing house. Today, staying true to this spirit, Collins books are packed with inspiration, innovation and practical expertise. They place you at the centre of a world of possibility and give you exactly what you need to explore it.

Collins. Freedom to teach

Published by Collins
An imprint of HarperCollinsPublishers
77 – 85 Fulham Palace Road
Hammersmith
London
W6 8JB

Browse the complete Collins catalogue at
www.collinseducation.com

10 9 8 7 6 5 4 3 2 1

ISBN 978 0 00 745740 3

British Library Cataloguing in Publication Data
A Catalogue record for this publication is available from the British Library

Commissioned by Andrew Campbell
Project managed by Alexandra Riley, Shirley Wakley and Charlie Evans
Production by Simon Moore

Designed by Jouve
Development by Lucien Jenkins
Edited by Rosalind Horton
Proofread by Sue Ecob
Indexed by Michael Forder
Illustrations by Ann Paganuzzi
Picture and text research by Grace Glendinning and Caroline Green
Cover picture research by Caroline Green
Cover design by Angela English
Technical review by Peter Callaghan

With special thanks to: Kimberley Atkins for devising the concept; Lucien Jenkins for additional authorial work.

Printed and bound by Printing Express Limited, Hong Kong

Cover: JOSEPH STALIN – 1948 USSR poster shows Stalin surrounded by admirers and the slogan 'Long Live The Komsomol Generation!' courtesy of Pictorial Press Ltd/Alamy

Acknowledgements
The publishers gratefully acknowledge the permission granted to reproduce the pictures and copyright material in this book. While every effort has been made to trace and contact copyright holders, where this has not been possible the publishers will be pleased to make the necessary arrangements at the first opportunity.

(t = top, b = bottom, c = centre, l = left, r = right)

Cover: Supplied by Pictorial Press Ltd/Alamy

pp 8, 10, 11, 12, 15t, 18tl, 18cr, 18cl, 18tr, 21, 23, 25, 57l & 67 Marxists Internet Archive; p 15bl Trotsky Internet Archive, a subarchive of the Marxists Internet Archive, by Sally Ryan in 1996; p 15br Encyclopedia of Trotskyism On-Line Transcribed, Edited & Formatted by Ted Crawford & David Walters; p 43l & 43r from *The Great Terror: A Reassessment*, by Robert Conquest © 2007: By permission of Oxford University Press; p 52 Jose Braz for the Marxists Internet Archive; p 57r from *On Stalin and Stalinism*, by Roy Medvedev © 1979: By permission of Oxford University Press.

p 38 Margaret Bourke-White/Time & Life Pictures/Getty Images; p 41 Hulton-Deutsch Collection/CORBIS; p 45 Kiev. Victor/Shutterstock; p 52 IgorGolovniov/Shutterstock; p 53t PARIS PIERCE/Alamy; p 53b Vladimir OKC/WikiMedia Commons; p 54 Leader, Teacher and Friend, 1937 (oil on canvas) by Shegal, Grigory Mikhailovich (1889-1956)/ Springville Museum of Art, Utah, USA/The Bridgeman Art Library; p 97 ITAR-TASS Photo Agency/Alamy.

MIX
Paper from responsible sources
FSC
www.fsc.org
FSC™ C007454

Contents

The establishment of Bolshevik rule

The Soviet Union in 1924

At the time of Lenin's death in 1924, Russia contained numerous nationalities, languages and religions. The majority of its inhabitants lived and worked in the countryside. Formerly an empire, it spread across Eastern Europe and central Asia, and had ports in the Baltic, Black Sea and Pacific.

About 90% worked in agriculture

About 10% worked in non-agricultural sector

Industrialisation in the early USSR

About 80% lived in the countryside

About 20% lived in towns and cities

Urbanisation in the early USSR

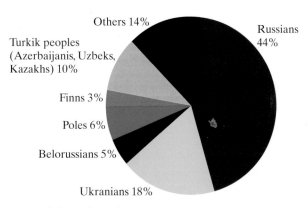

Others 14%

Russians 44%

Turkik peoples (Azerbaijanis, Uzbeks, Kazakhs) 10%

Finns 3%

Poles 6%

Belorussians 5%

Ukranians 18%

Nationalities in the early USSR

Government and politics

The last reigning Tsar (emperor), Nicholas II, had headed a government in which there was no system of legal restraint on his power. By the time of Lenin's death in 1924, the Soviet Union had become a one-party state. This one-party state had key institutions of political control:

- political parties other than the Bolsheviks were banned
- political opponents were arrested
- rebellions were savagely put down
- the Communist Party's authority was upheld by the *Cheka*.

A ban on factions (groups campaigning on individual issues) within the Bolshevik Party was passed in 1921. Although ostensibly a measure to ensure unity within the party, the ban stifled debate. After 1921, it was not possible openly to criticise the party leadership.

The legal system was placed under political control and became an ideological tool. Purges and show trials were held, and Lenin established labour camps to house political opponents of his regime. By 1924, 315 labour camps, known as *gulags*, were in place.

Lenin's readiness to use force and terror to control both the country and the party paved the way for the Stalinist dictatorship of the 1930s.

The economy

In 1921, at the end of the civil war, Lenin ended War Communism, which had been introduced in 1918 to:

- nationalise industry and make private enterprise illegal
- introduce central planning and direction of the economy
- seize grain from peasants to feed towns and troops.

War Communism may have helped win the civil war, but it had led to economic decline and resentment. The New Economic Policy (NEP) was a pragmatic change of direction that introduced a mixed economy in which some statecontrol was retained but private enterprise was reintroduced:

- Major industries like coal, steel, railways and banks remained state monopolies.
- Private trading and the private ownership of small businesses were legalised.
- The state stopped requisitioning (seizing) grain, and instead peasants handed over to the state a fixed proportion of the grain they produced; in 1924 that in turn gave way to money payments.

Since the party's economic policies were creating a powerful opposition, Lenin ordered an ideological retreat. War Communism was replaced with the NEP. Lenin introduced the NEP to:

- prevent famine
- encourage economic recovery
- end rural discontent
- feed the urban population.

This pragmatic decision brought economic recovery. Agriculture produced enough food both for the peasants and for the urban proletariat. Industrial production recovered and exceeded pre-war levels.

A side effect was the emergence of a new social group. Known as NEPmen, these were people who had grown wealthy under the NEP. This was bound to be controversial and divisive, as the Bolsheviks were supposed to be overthrowing the economic rule of bourgeoisie and factory owners, as much as the political rule of Tsars and nobles.

Examiners' notes

The NEP was still in existence at the beginning of the period you are studying, so you need to know about it. (see pages 16–19.)

Continued on the next two pages

Introduction: Russia in the early 20th century

Essential notes

Karl Marx developed the political theory that bears his name: Marxism. With Friedrich Engels he wrote *Das Kapital* (1867) and the *Communist Manifesto* (1848), which presented ideas on historical development and criticised the capitalist economy and the system of government that went with it.

Essential notes

St Petersburg had its German-sounding name changed to Petrograd in 1914, following Russia's entry into World War I. The name changed again to Leningrad after Lenin's death in 1924.

Essential notes

Before the revolution, Russia used the Julian calendar, which placed its dates several days behind those in Western Europe. That is why you will find some texts date the Russian Revolution to October and others to November. In January 1918, Russia formally adopted the Gregorian calendar and 31 January 1918 became 14 February 1918. The Edexcel Specification now refers to the 'March Revolution' and the 'November Revolution'.

Politics and culture

Lenin had realised early on that society could be controlled not just through use of the Secret Police, but also through the manipulation of culture. Authors, poets and artists now had to espouse the values of revolutionary Russia.

Politics and the family

The family unit and the institution of marriage were attacked as bourgeois notions. The Bolsheviks legislated for equality for women, but in fact few women reached positions of authority within the party. By 1924, Lenin was expressing doubts over the party's policy towards the family.

Communist ideology

Lenin had a vision of Russian society based on the ideas of the German philosopher Karl Marx. Marx believed that human society developed through a series of stages, each dominated by a particular social class. Lenin had to adapt Marxism to suit Russian conditions. Marx had assumed revolution would take place in industrialised countries, while Russia in 1917 was largely agrarian with a peasant population. However, he had been surprised to notice that even in his lifetime sales of his most famous work *Capital* had been better in Russia than anywhere else in the world.

The Marxist Russian Social Democratic Party had split into two groups in part over their interpretation of this aspect of Marx. Lenin took the view that Russia needed a small, dedicated and disciplined group of revolutionaries to push events forward to a crisis, and that the industrial proletariat and the rural peasantry would never achieve change without this leadership.

During the 1917 Revolution, Tsar Nicholas II abdicated and, initially, a coalition, the Provisional Government, took power. It was overthrown in its turn by the Bolsheviks later the same year. A civil war followed, which the Bolsheviks won partly because their enemies were divided. Throughout all this, Lenin's leadership was never in question. As a result, his illness and death left the ruling party with a crisis: who was going to be the new leader?

Feudal society is ruled by a monarchy and the aristocracy, who oppress the peasants. The final stage of feudalism is a bourgeois revolution led by the newly developed middle class.

Capitalist society is ruled by the middle classes (or bourgeoisie), who exploit the workers (or proletariat). The final stage of capitalism is a 'proletarian' revolution by the industrial urban working class.

Socialist society is ruled by the working classes for the good of the whole of society. The state takes over the running of the economy.

Communist society has no social classes; there is social equality and the state withers away to leave true freedom.

Marx's theory of the development and structure of societies

March Tsar Nicholas II abdicates. The Provisional Government (a coalition of Liberals, Mensheviks and Social Revolutionaries) takes power.

The Russian Civil War begins between the Reds (the Bolsheviks) and the Whites (disunited collection of anti-Bolshevik groups); War Communism is introduced.

Lenin ends War Communism and introduces the New Economic Policy to allow the economy to recover.

1917	1918	1919	1920	1921	1922	1923	1924

November Lenin leads the Bolshevik Revolution. The Bolsheviks seize power from the Provisional Government, working through the Petrograd Soviet.

The Bolsheviks win the Civil War, but Russia is economically devastated.

Lenin suffers a series of strokes, leaving him unable to lead the Communist Party effectively.

Lenin dies in January leaving a power vacuum. The power struggle begins.

Timeline of key events, 1917–24

The structure of government in the USSR included a series of committees called, in Russian, 'soviets', from which the state gained its name. The electoral process began at the grassroots with the local committees, and worked upwards through a system of delegates to the committees which, in theory, ran the country. As a one-party state, membership of the governmental system was limited to party members.

Essential notes

The Whites were aided by Western powers. This helps to explain Stalin's later distrust of the West.

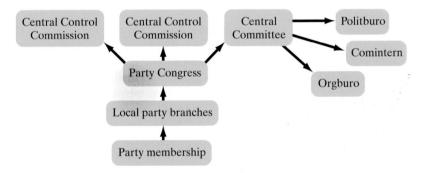

The structure of government in the USSR

Stalin and the power struggle

Stalin was born Josef Vissaronovich Dzhugashvili in Georgia in 1879. Although he came from a peasant family, he received an education. Following his discovery of the writings of Lenin, he joined the Bolshevik Party in 1903. By 1912 he was made a member of the Central Committee of the Bolshevik Party. Clearly demonstrating a ruthless streak, he robbed banks to help with party funds, covertly disseminated Bolshevik literature and organised underground cells.

Stalin and Lenin

Stalin adopted Lenin's policies after the latter had returned to Russia in April 1917. Stalin did not play a key role in either the October Revolution of 1917 or the civil war.

Stalin formed a close relationship with Lenin, following their first meeting in 1905. In a group of middle- and upper-class intellectuals, Stalin looked more like the authentic face of the working class. On one occasion Lenin described Stalin as 'that wonderful Georgian'. Lenin's trust in Stalin continued until December 1922, when he began to fear that Stalin was taking over the party and wrote to Trotsky asking for his help. Lenin was sharply critical of Stalin in his *Testament*, urging other party members to replace him with a less abrasive person.

Stalin's personality

Stalin was known as a diligent organiser and an efficient bureaucrat, prepared to undertake the routine tasks other leading figures of the party were unwilling to do. He was unmemorable, being described by one Menshevik as a 'grey blur', and as 'an industrious mediocrity' and 'comrade card-index' by members of the Politburo (the principal policy-making committee of the Communist Party). He had a reputation for brutality, stemming in part from the way in which he had carried out Lenin's orders (to the extent that Lenin himself had reprimanded him). Yet in political terms he was on neither the 'right' or 'left' of the party. He could thus appear as a moderating influence during heated ideological debates. During the power struggle Stalin proved himself both politically astute and manipulative, and appealed to Russian patriotism.

Stalin's posts and powerbase

Stalin's powerbase rested on his positions within the party. In 1919, Stalin was made head of the *Orgburo* and elected to the new *Politburo,* the main organ of power. These promotions were soon followed by his appointment in 1922 as the party's first Secretary-General in charge of party organisation. These posts gave him the power of patronage and hence significant influence over the lower and middle ranks of the party. He was now able to control the party organisation by cramming Party Congresses with delegates who would vote as he directed. As a result, some

Comrade Stalin, having become Secretary General has unlimited authority concentrated in his hands and I am not sure whether he will always be capable of using that authority with sufficient caution ... Stalin is too rude and this defect ... becomes inolerable in a Secretary-General. That is why I suggest the comrades think about a way of removing Stalin from that post and appointing another man ... who in all other respects differs from Comrade Stalin in having only one advantage, namely, that of being more tolerant, more loyal, more polite and more considerate to the comrades.

Lenin's *Testament*

in the leadership saw him as a valuable ally in their own ambitions, failing to realise that he was a powerful rival.

Similarly, through his position in the party, Stalin was able to control party membership. He brought in the Leninsty, new members recruited during the Lenin Enrolment of 1924–5:

- party membership virtually doubled to one million
- the majority were drawn from the urban proletariat and peasants
- most were young, inexperienced and poorly educated
- as such, they were malleable and likely to obey Stalin's directions.

Stalin also worked to expel militant groups within the party such as students and soldiers. These were more likely to support Trotsky and the Left Opposition in any leadership contest.

Lenin also appointed Stalin People's Commissar for Nationalities in 1917. Stalin was brutal in his treatment of the ethnic minorities under his control. Stalin's ruthless conduct in the forcible 'Sovietisation' of Georgia should have alerted other contenders in the leadership struggle to Stalin's real nature.

Essential notes

Orgburo is an abbreviation for the Organisational Bureau of the Central Committee of the Communist Party. It oversaw the organisation of the Communist Party, supervising the work of local party committees and appointing party members to key positions of influence.

1917: People's Commissar for Nationalities	Controlled all non-Russian nationalities in the regions that made up the USSR. He was responsible for over 50 million people.
1919: Head of *Orgburo*	Enabled him to make appointments within the party. He could therefore fill important posts such as regional and local party secretaries with his followers.
1919: Head of the Workers' and Peasants' Inspectorate	Directed and supervised the running of all government departments. Able to investigate the background and practices of every official.
1921: Head of Central Control Commission	Stalin had the power to remove party officials from their posts. He used this position to expel not only corrupt party cadres but also members who did not support him.
1922: Secretary-General of the Party	Supervised the day-to-day running of the *Politburo*, including meeting agendas and discussion documents. This gave him control over the flow to the *Politburo* members.

Stalin's posts and powerbase within the party structure

Like the Soviet state, the Communist Party operated through a system of elections to committees. The electorate here was the membership of the party.

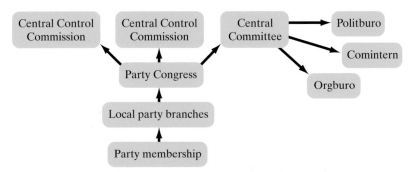

The Communist party structure was revised several times in the period 1924–53: this is a simplified account

Stalin's rivals in the power struggle: the left

Trotsky

Trotsky was born in 1879 to a prosperous, middle-class, Jewish family. By 1896, he had become a Marxist. He became acquainted with Lenin during his exile in London in 1902. Following the 1903 split in the Russian Social Democratic Labour Party (RSDLP), he joined the Mensheviks.

Trotsky, revolution and civil war

Trotsky joined the Bolshevik Party early in 1917 and during the leadership struggle was seen by some as a latecomer, not a true Bolshevik. Nevertheless, his contribution to the Bolshevik seizure of power was second only to that of Lenin's. He planned the October Revolution (1917); his organisation of the Red Army helped assure the Bolshevik victory in the Russian Civil War 1918–21.

Trotsky and Lenin

Trotsky did not always get on with Lenin. They clashed over issues of ideology. But Lenin supported Trotsky in key decisions, for example siding with Trotsky against Stalin over the use of Tsarist army officers during the civil war. Trotsky in turn supported Lenin in key policy decisions. Despite having ideological qualms, for instance, Trotsky supported Lenin's controversial introduction of the NEP (though he later turned against the policy).

Trotsky's personality

Trotsky was popular with the younger members of the party and university students, who appreciated his intellect. His oratory and military leadership during the civil war won him much support in the armed forces.

Some party members considered him to be arrogant, aloof and disrespectful. Many feared that his uncompromising views would divide the party in the event of Lenin's death. Zinoviev and Kamenev feared that Trotsky wanted to become dictator. Senior Bolsheviks will have been aware that during the years of the French Revolution (which began 1789), leadership of the country was seized by a leading general, Napoleon. Karl Marx had warned against such 'Bonapartism' and opponents of Trotsky had feared he would follow the Bonaparte model.

Trotsky placed himself above routine politics; he was not interested in tactical political alliances or intrigue.

> Comrade Trotsky… is distinguished not only by outstanding ability. He is personally perhaps the most capable man in the present Central Committee, but he has displayed excessive self-assurance…
>
> Lenin's *Testament*

| Commissar for War | Control over the Red Army, the only institution capable of overthrowing the communist government |

Trotsky's posts and powerbase

Zinoviev

Gregory Zinoviev was the son of a Jewish dairy farmer in the Ukraine. He joined the Bolshevik Party in 1903. Following his arrest in 1907 for revolutionary activities against the Tsarist state, he was exiled to Switzerland. Here he became closely associated with Lenin.

Zinoviev, revolution and civil war

Zinoviev did not support the October Revolution. He favoured a coalition with other socialist groups including the Mensheviks. During the civil war he ensconced himself in a luxury hotel in Leningrad, far away from the action.

Zinoviev and Lenin

Zinoviev was Lenin's oldest and at times closest associate. However, his disagreements with Lenin over the October Revolution and the nature of a post-revolutionary government led to a temporary cooling of relations.

> … the October episode with Zinoviev and Kamenev was, of course, no accident, but neither can the blame for it be laid upon them personally …
>
> Lenin's *Testament*

Zinoviev's personality

Zinoviev was seen as vain, inept and craven. Leading communists were contemptuous of his failure to support Lenin's decision to launch the October Revolution.

Head of the Leningrad branch of the Communist Party	In charge of the Communist Party in one of the Soviet Union's two major cities and the birthplace of the Russian Revolution.
Head of the *Comintern*	Coordinated and directed Communist Parties in other countries.

Zinoviev's posts and powerbase

Kamenev

Lev Kamenev was born in 1883 and was a full-time revolutionary and Bolshevik from 1905. He was expelled from school for seditious activity and exiled on several occasions, eventually joining Stalin in exile in Siberia.

Kamenev, revolution and civil war

Kamenev did not support the October Revolution and wanted a post-revolutionary socialist coalition. He played no role in the civil war.

Kamenev and Lenin

Kamenev was a close associate of Lenin's 1907–17 when exiled abroad and would engage Lenin in passionate debates over party doctrine. He lost influence with Lenin after opposing the April Theses on ideological grounds and, later, the revolution.

Kamenev's personality

He was regarded as both able and reliable, and certainly more intellectually competent than Zinoviev. But he lacked a clear vision of a socialist society or the ability to inspire.

Essential notes

Lenin argued in the April Theses, upon his return to Russia in April 1917, that the Bolsheviks should no longer support the Provisional Government. Instead, revolutionaries should encourage the people of Russia to take control of the country.

Head of the Moscow branch of the Communist Party	In charge of the Communist Party in the Soviet Union's new capital, Moscow.
Chairman of the Central Committee	Headed the body that elected members of the Politburo.

Kamenev's posts and powerbase

Stalin's rivals in the power struggle: the right

Nicolai Bukharin

A rising star of the party, Bukharin was born into a lower-middle-class family in 1888. Becoming a Bolshevik in 1906, he was arrested and sent into internal exile in 1911. He fled the country and while abroad met Lenin in 1912.

Bukharin, revolution and civil war

Bukharin played a prominent role in the pre-1917 Bolshevik Party. After the October Revolution in Petrograd, he led revolutionaries in the future capital city, Moscow, in seizing power. During the civil war, he contributed to *Pravda*, the party's newspaper, urging the Reds on to victory.

Bukharin and Lenin

Lenin regarded Bukharin as an important political theorist. However, Bukharin often argued with Lenin about party doctrine. For example, he initially refused to support the NEP, which he saw as an ideological retreat. However, Bukharin later abandoned his early radicalism to support Lenin's NEP, becoming its most strident advocate.

> Bukharin is not only a most valuable and major theorist of the party; he is also rightly considered the favourite of the whole party, but his theoretical views can be classified as fully Marxist only with the great reserve…
>
> Lenin's *Testament*

Bukharin's personality

Bukharin was one of the party's intellectuals, with cultural interests well beyond politics. He seems to have been liked even by rivals within the party. However, he did not have Stalin's political talent for plotting.

Bukharin's posts and powerbase

Bukharin had support in Moscow given his early work there in the days after the October Revolution. This increased after Kamenev was dismissed from his post as Party Secretary in 1927. He was popular among the youth of the party.

His strength derived from his popularity within the party and his standing as an exceptional political theorist. His book *The ABC of Communism* was considered the most useful guide to understanding party ideology. He was also editor of two influential newspapers, *Pravda* and *Communist*. He was therefore able to influence both party and public opinion.

However, this was not a powerbase that could readily translate into practical support. Although widely liked and respected, Bukharin was not able to call out supporters when he needed them in the effective way that Stalin could.

Popular within the party	Gave Bukharin a broad base of support within the party. But this was difficult to quantify and draw on in a political struggle.
Leading political theorist	Respect within the party but no control over any aspect of the party machine.

Bukharin's posts and powerbase

Other figures on the right

In addition to the main contenders in the power struggle, there were several others who had notable posts and powerbases. Two key figures on the right of the party formed an alliance with Bukharin.

Rykov

Alexei Rykov was born in 1881 to a peasant family. He rose quickly in the party to become chairman of the *Vesenkha* (Supreme Economic Council) and later was chairman of the *Sovnarkom* (Council of People's Commissars). He was gruff and opinionated, qualities that did not win him many allies in the party. His reputation for heavy drinking was commonplace knowledge. Like Bukharin he was a fervent exponent of the NEP.

Tomsky

Born in 1880, Mikhail Tomsky was prominent in the trade union movement and a committed delegate of the metalworkers' union. After 1918 he was chairman of the Central Council of Trade Unions. He clashed with Lenin over the diminution of the trade unions' role in the new Soviet government, dismayed that trade unions were no longer considered integral to the creation of socialist society.

Summary: Left and right

Left

Because of the nature of the power struggle, the key strengths of the rivals became weaknesses. Trotsky's command of the army seemed menacing, and so alienated the very individuals among the left of the leadership he needed as his allies. By contrast, Kamenev and Zinoviev were too inexperienced in military affairs. This undermined their claim to be leadership material for a country with enemies.

Stalin was less prominent than these three famous Bolsheviks, but he could not be accused of any of their failings.

Right

Stalin understood the nature of the competition for leadership and his rivals did not. Bukharin clearly thought of it as a debate over policy. Stalin realised it was a power struggle. Where Bukharin wanted to win arguments, Stalin ensured he won votes.

Essential notes

The *Vesenkha* was formed in 1917. It was the first governmental organisation established to plan and manage the economy, especially industry. It oversaw the nationalised industries (coal, steel and railways). Later it played a role in the management of the Five-Year Plans. In this capacity it often came into conflict with *Gosplan* (see page 19).

Essential notes

Sovnarkom was created in 1917. It formed the new government following the October Revolution. Its influence began to decline after 1921.

Examiners' notes

Be careful when you are learning about the negative aspects of other contenders that you don't give the impression that Stalin was the only possible winner. Draw up a chart comparing Trotsky, Zinoviev, Kamenev and Bukharin with a column for positive qualities as well as the negatives.

Examiners' notes

As you think about the reasons why Stalin won the power struggle, remember the background debates. Notice how Stalin positions himself and takes on the point of view, whether it be socialism in one country or the rejection of the NEP, which resonates with the whole party.

World revolution or socialism in one country

Interpretations of Leninism

Lenin had led the Bolsheviks to power in October 1917, and his ideas and principles guided the party until his death in 1924. Even after his death, the leading contenders for power claimed to adhere to Leninism. Nevertheless, there was little consensus about precisely what Leninism stood for, and Lenin's ideas were subject to competing interpretations, which caused splits in the party.

Lenin's radical ideas and policies, so apparent during the early years of Bolshevik rule, inspired the left of the party to:

- push forward with revoutionary changes to society and the economy
- abolish capitalism
- abolish currency
- abolish private property
- enforce War Communism during the civil war.

Lenin's later policies, with an emphasis to gradual change and the introduction of the NEP, were favoured by the right of the party.

The person most associated with the left of the party was Trotsky. He was joined in 1925 by Zinoviev and Kamenev. Initially hostile to the NEP, Bukharin took up a position on the right or moderate wing. Throughout much of the 1920s Stalin occupied the centre ground, pragmatically adopting policies as conditions in the USSR changed.

World revolution

The left of the party, notably Trotsky, believed in the theory of world revolution. This entailed the following beliefs:

- The communist revolution in Russia was bound to fail because the urban working class or proletariat was too underdeveloped and too small to complete the task. The majority of the population were still peasants with little revolutionary inclination.
- Russia did not have the economic resources to complete the transition to socialism.
- Russia needed the assistance of the working classes in more economically advanced countries, such as Germany or Great Britain.
- Every effort should be made to help the proletariat in these countries to enact their own revolutions.
- Communist regimes in these industrialised, advanced countries would then provide the USSR with the resources necessary to complete the building of socialism.
- Russians should keep on fighting until a world revolution was a reality.

Trotsky also wanted the Communist Party to push the Soviet Union in a more radical direction with labour units organised in a military fashion, complete with military discipline, and the forcible collectivisation of the peasants. In this way, his theory of world revolution dovetailed neatly with his calls for the abolition of the NEP and the introduction of a programme of rapid industrialisation. It would have the added advantage of eliminating old and outmoded ways of thought, putting society firmly on a socialist footing.

Socialism in one country

The right of the party argued that socialism should be firmly established in the Soviet Union. Socialism in one country was a theory put forward by Stalin in the last months of 1924, elaborated upon by Bukharin in 1925 and finally adopted as state policy.

This position represented a tactical change of direction for Stalin, who had begun 1924 still arguing that a socialist revolution in one country was wholly unsatisfactory. His change of heart was apparent in a January 1926 article, *On the Issues of Leninism*:

'What is meant by the possibility of the victory of socialism in one country? It means the ... possibility of the proletariat seizing power and using that power to build a complete socialist society in our country ...'

As a policy, socialism in one country meant:

- World revolution had failed: in 1919, a revolution in Germany and a Bolshevik experiment in Hungary had both collapsed.
- The peoples of the Soviet Union could solve their own problems and build a mighty workers' state to rival the capitalist West.
- The continuing existence of the Soviet Union was paramount, even if this meant abandoning the idea of world revolution.

Stalin effectively appealed to Russian patriotism when he said it was possible to build socialism in the USSR. But socialism in one country was a malleable policy that allowed the Communist Party to dictate the best way to achieve socialism, given conditions in the country at the time.

Stalin claimed that socialism in one country was faithful to Lenin's ideas and condemned the audacity of Trotsky's world revolution as a threat to the security of the USSR, which many in the party feared was threatened by imminent invasion by Western capitalist nations. By successfully appealing to Russian nationalism, Stalin was able to portray Trotsky as an isolated figure, out of touch with the mood of the party.

The completion of the socialist revolution within national limits is unthinkable.

Trotsky

Can socialism *possibly* be established in one country alone by that country's unaided strength? This question must be answered in the affirmative.

Stalin

Left and right wings in the ideological power struggle

Examiners' notes

Understanding the ideological arguments is a good way of getting to grips with the power struggle. Make sure you know what views the contenders held on these key issues and how these affected their levels of support in the party.

NEP and the industrialisation debate

What was the NEP?

NEP (New Economic Policy) was a key policy issue dividing the party hierarchy in the mid-1920s. The debate was:

- Practical: how the government should manage the economy.
- Ideological: what sort of society the USSR was to be.

In turn, this economic debate shaped the struggle for leadership. The NEP was conceived by Lenin to introduce a 'mixed economy' to allow Russia to recover from the economic consequences of the civil war. It:

- abolished workers' committees and reintroduced managers
- replaced grain requisitioning with a 'tax in kind' on grain
- allowed peasants to sell their surplus grain at market for a profit
- returned small businesses to private ownership
- legalised profit
- reintroduced payments
- retained larger industries, such as railways, mining and steel, in state control.

NEP in 1924

In 1924 the communist government moved from the 'tax in kind', under which peasants handed over a proportion of the grain and other agricultural produce they had grown, to a system of money payments.

In 1924 economic growth was still robust and the NEP allowed the USSR to recover from the devastation of the civil war. By 1925, however, practical problems with the NEP became evident.

Lenin stressed that the NEP was a temporary measure. By the middle of the 1920s, economic conditions had shifted, with industrial and agricultural production both recovering:

Essential notes

The graph shows production expressed as a percentage of what it had been in 1913.

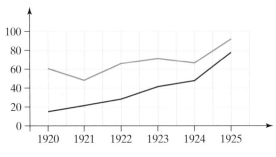

— Industrial production

— Grain production

Economic recovery under the NEP

Effects of the NEP

The NEP significantly altered economy and society within the Soviet Union.

Essential notes

The NEP debate was an important part of the struggle for leadership, as you will see on pages 20–21. The stages of the power struggle are marked by shifting alliances supporting or opposing the NEP.

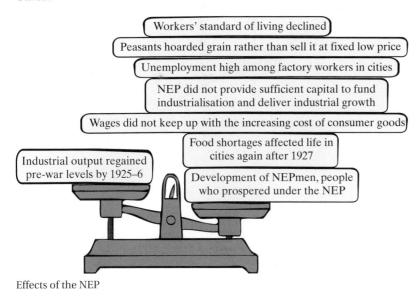

Workers' standard of living declined

Peasants hoarded grain rather than sell it at fixed low price

Unemployment high among factory workers in cities

NEP did not provide sufficient capital to fund industrialisation and deliver industrial growth

Wages did not keep up with the increasing cost of consumer goods

Food shortages affected life in cities again after 1927

Industrial output regained pre-war levels by 1925–6

Development of NEPmen, people who prospered under the NEP

Effects of the NEP

Problems with the NEP

After 1925 serious problems began to emerge and increasingly the NEP came under attack.

The left of the party was uneasy at the revival of capitalism, even in the guise of 'state capitalism'. The growth of a new class of rich peasants and businessmen, together with an increase in prostitution and other social vices, was seen as the consequence of the NEP. Thus the NEP became increasingly unattractive on ideological grounds.

The memory of war and the fear that capitalist countries were about to attack the Soviet Union again added urgency to the argument in favour of rapid industrialisation, especially after 1928. This fear undermined support for the NEP among the party hierarchy. It was also decisively to shape the Five-Year Plans that began at this time, continually ensuring that armaments and industries that were important for the military were given more importance than consumer goods.

This was the backdrop to the struggle for leadership. The debate over the nature of industrialisation and the continuation of the NEP split the party between the left and the right. Groups within the party lined up to support different candidates in part according to how they stood on the NEP.

Essential notes

It is easy to dismiss the NEP as an outright failure because the party voted with Stalin to get rid of it in 1928. However, it had served a useful economic purpose and might have continued to do so given more time. The timing of Stalin's decision to argue against it shows his skill as an opportunist – it made sense to highlight the grain procurement crisis now that his only remaining rival was Bukharin.

Continued on the next two pages

Examiners' notes

When answering questions on the leadership struggle and the NEP, give examples of Stalin's opportunism, and the flexibility of thinking that allowed him to outwit rivals. His rivals were cleverer, but being more ideologically principled made them more inflexible.

Essential notes

Kulak was the word coined to describe those peasants who had become prosperous, some under earlier Tsarist economic reforms, others during the NEP.

Examiners' notes

You need to be clear about the ideological struggle. To make sure you understand it, you could try drawing up a chart summarising left- and right-wing views on the three big issues explained in the text (Leninism, world revolution or socialism in one country, NEP) and note down the main figures on each side.

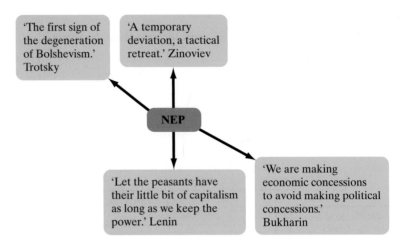

'The first sign of the degeneration of Bolshevism.' Trotsky

'A temporary deviation, a tactical retreat.' Zinoviev

NEP

'Let the peasants have their little bit of capitalism as long as we keep the power.' Lenin

'We are making economic concessions to avoid making political concessions.' Bukharin

Key individuals' comments on the NEP

Left demands rapid industrialisation

The left wing of the party, led by Trotsky, Zinoviev and Kamenev, distrusted the NEP:

- Practical: it was economically imprudent, and would lead to social division and economic chaos.

- Ideological: it was ideologically unsound, a departure from Marxist analysis.

Instead of creating a workers' state, the NEP allowed peasants (a class held in much disdain by Marx) and businessmen to grow richer while the urban proletariat (industrial workers) became poorer.

The left wanted to end the NEP immediately and focus on rapid industrialisation. Supported by the radical economist Preobrazhensky, they wanted to force the peasants to pay for industrialisation through a resumption of grain requisitioning. Their main target was the rich peasant, for whom the insulting label *kulak* had been coined (literally 'fist' in Russian, and a reference to their alleged fist-like hold on the peasants; see page 26).

Right demands gradual socialism

The right wing of the party, led by Bukharin, believed that the NEP should last for a generation. They believed that the NEP was creating economic stability and was evidence of a workers' and peasants' alliance. Socialism should develop gradually.

Bukharin and the right wanted to encourage the peasants to become richer, so that they would spend more on consumer goods, which would, in turn, lead to the growth of the manufacturing industry. They believed that conflict with the peasants would lead to economic collapse, endangering the development of a communist society.

Stalin and the NEP

In 1921, Stalin approved Lenin's policy of the NEP. In 1923 Trotsky and other members of the left were highly critical of *Gosplan* for its 'flagrant radical errors of economic policy'. In the spirit of Lenin's ban on factionalism, this allowed Stalin to portray Trotsky as so intent on opposing the NEP that he was willing to destroy party unity.

Stalin supported the NEP for practical reasons: to feed the country and deliver the industrialisation that everyone agreed was necessary. By 1928, when it was clear that the policy had not delivered the anticipated industrial growth, he abandoned first the NEP and then his alliance with Bukharin and the right. Bukharin may have seen Stalin as an 'unprincipled intriguer', but others saw his change of opinion on the NEP as pragmatic and it won him support in the party.

Essential notes

Gosplan was the government body responsible for economic planning in the USSR.

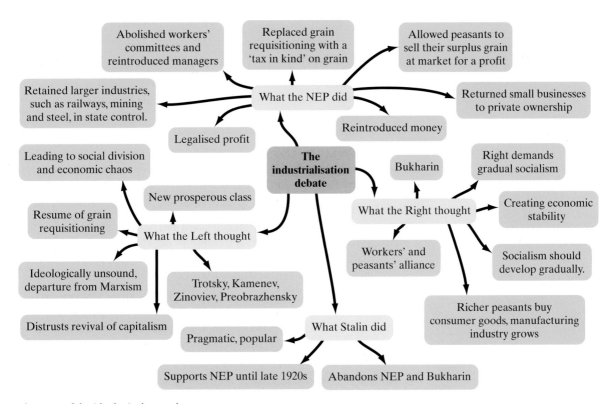

Elements of the ideological struggle

Essential notes

A *troika* is a traditional Russian sledge or carriage drawn by three horses. The term is used to describe the political alliance between Zinoviev, Kamenev and Stalin. You may also meet the term 'triumvirate', which means a leadership committee of three people.

The stages of the power struggle

The position in 1921–2

Stalin's party positions, acquired while Lenin was still alive, concentrated considerable power in his hands. His rivals' failure to recognise this led them initially to dismiss him as a serious contender.

Lenin introduced the Ban on Factions in 1921 as a way of suppressing dissent and division within the party in the aftermath of the civil war. The punishment for factionalism was expulsion from the party. Anyone who criticised official policies could be accused of factionalism. The Ban on Factions gave Stalin, who could already control votes at party congresses, a significant advantage in the power struggle.

Stage 1: Defeat of the Left Opposition (1923–5)

Stalin, Zinoviev and Kamenev formed their *troika* alliance in 1923. They wanted to exclude Trotsky from power. As head of the Red Army, Trotsky was the man most feared by the other contenders. Trotsky himself formed the Left Opposition to counter the *troika's* policies.

Stalin's actions

Stalin let Zinoviev and Kamenev attack Trotsky while he himself often took a very moderate position in public. For example, in 1925 he opposed moves by Zinoviev and Kamenev to have Trotsky expelled from the party.

Behind the scenes he continued to fill the party bodies and gatherings with his supporters to block Trotsky's policies. Stalin defended the NEP and presented the Left Opposition as factionalists.

Mistakes of Stalin's opponents

Zinoviev and Kamenev underestimated Stalin and believed Trotsky to be the real threat. In May 1924 the Central Committee decided not to publish Lenin's *Testament*. Zinoviev and Kamenev felt that publication would benefit Trotsky by weakening their ally, Stalin. Trotsky himself did not insist on publication.

Trotsky published *The Lessons of October* (1924) attacking Zinoviev and Kamenev for failing to support the October Revolution. In these increasingly bitter disputes, the competing groups and individuals were weakening one another. Meanwhile Stalin, appearing to be above the fray, seemed increasingly statesmanlike.

Zinoviev and Kamenev retaliated, accusing Trotsky of disloyalty to Lenin by emphasising his role in 1917 at Lenin's expense. Condemned by the Central Committee in January 1925, Trotsky lost his position as Commissar for War and thus his powerbase.

Policy issues

The right and many moderates in the centre decided that Trotsky's anti-NEP stance and his belief in world revolution were hostile to Lenin's ideas. Socialism in one country was viewed as more Leninist. Trotsky's world revolution made him appear negative and unpatriotic by suggesting that socialism in the Soviet Union alone was not possible.

Stage 2: Defeat of the United Opposition (1925–7)

With Trotsky weakened, the *troika* had no common enemy. Stalin's newly-adopted policy of socialism in one country seemed to complement the NEP.

Stalin's actions

Stalin now turned against Zinoviev and Kamenev. He formed a new alliance with Bukharin and the right to defeat his former allies. By appearing pro-NEP he continued to appear moderate.

Mistakes of Stalin's opponents

In 1925 Zinoviev and Kamenev attacked Stalin and his new ally Bukharin. They called for a no-confidence vote at the 14th Party Congress, but Stalin's supporters easily defeated this motion. This is a clear example of Stalin's success in building up a powerbase that could vote as an organised block at key moments.

In 1926 Zinoviev and Kamenev formed the United Opposition with Trotsky. This appeared cynically opportunistic given the evident hostility between the three in stage 1. Zinoviev and Kamenev lost their positions in Leningrad and Moscow; all three were expelled from the party. Trotsky was expelled from the USSR in 1929.

Policy issues

Debates over the efficacy of the NEP formed the backdrop to stage 2. Zinoviev and Kamenev called for an end to the NEP, in favour of rapid industrialisation. In order to defeat the left, Stalin lent his support to the continuation of the NEP. In reality, Stalin believed the NEP to be ineffectual.

Stage 3: Defeat of the Right Opposition (1928–9)

Having defeated the left, Stalin confronted the right in 1928.

Stalin's actions

Stalin came out in favour of rapid industrialisation and against the NEP. In abandoning the NEP, Stalin revealed his opportunism. Yet the majority in the party, who also favoured an end to the NEP, saw his change of mind as pragmatic and sensible.

Mistakes of Stalin's opponents

All the rivals for the leadership could see that, despite Lenin's ban, the power struggle had created factions. Bukharin knew that the right's policy of socialism in one country had triumphed over the left's campaign for world revolution. He assumed that this meant the right could successfully defend the NEP against its critics on the left; at the 1929 Party Congress he attempted to do so. Stalin moved his supporters to vote against him. Bukharin was then removed from the *Politburo* and the *Comintern*, which he had headed since Zinoviev's defeat.

Examiners' notes

Be careful with these stages of the struggle. While it makes it easier for us to understand the events if we categorise them neatly like this, it was nothing like as clear cut at the time. Don't fall into the trap of thinking Stalin master-minded it this way from the outset.

'Stalin knows only one method… to plant a knife in the back.'

Bukharin complaining to Kamenev, 1928

Essential notes

The industrialisation debate is central here. By 1927 problems with the NEP made Stalin's position seem increasingly reasonable. From January 1928 he led a campaign of forcible grain requisitioning that ultimately resulted in the policy of collectivisation by 1929 (see page 24).

Why Stalin won the leadership struggle

By 1929 Stalin's victory was assured.

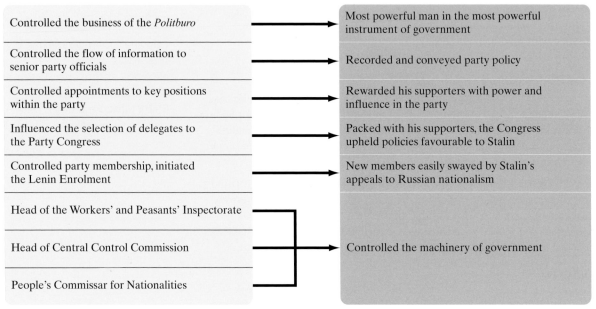

Controlled the business of the *Politburo*	Most powerful man in the most powerful instrument of government
Controlled the flow of information to senior party officials	Recorded and conveyed party policy
Controlled appointments to key positions within the party	Rewarded his supporters with power and influence in the party
Influenced the selection of delegates to the Party Congress	Packed with his supporters, the Congress upheld policies favourable to Stalin
Controlled party membership, initiated the Lenin Enrolment	New members easily swayed by Stalin's appeals to Russian nationalism
Head of the Workers' and Peasants' Inspectorate	
Head of Central Control Commission	Controlled the machinery of government
People's Commissar for Nationalities	

Stalin's growing power

Stalin's victory had been achieved through a combination of different factors.

Stalin's positions within the party

Stalin's positions as Secretary-General and Head of the *Orgburo* within a centralised party machine concentrated more power in Stalin's hands than his rivals realised, including control over membership and discussions.

Mistakes and misjudgements of others

Political rivals did not see Stalin as a threat. Zinoviev, Kamenev and other senior figures feared that Trotsky wanted to seize control of the revolution and become dictator of the Soviet Union. It did not occur to them that Stalin might do so. This collective fear and suspicion of Trotsky contributed to the decision by senior party members not to publish Lenin's *Testament*, which would have ended Stalin's political career.

Each of the other contenders made individual mistakes:

Trotsky did not attend Lenin's funeral, making him appear disrespectful to Lenin's memory at a time when a personality cult had already begun. In contrast, Stalin was a pallbearer, gave the eulogy and thus posed as Lenin's natural successor. Trotsky became increasingly vulnerable to the charge of factionalism, especially after the 13th Party Congress in 1924. He was finally expelled from the party as a factionalist.

Trotsky did not have the political will to defeat Stalin. While he had a powerbase in the Red Army he did not use it and, when this was removed, he was not popular enough in the party to sustain an attack on Stalin.

Zinoviev and **Kamenev** allowed Stalin to fill committees and the Party Congress with his supporters during stage 1 of the power struggle. They did not realise the potential power of Stalin's administrative positions.

Their attempt, as part of the United Opposition, to mobilise the masses, taking the struggle to the streets in stage 2, opened them up to the charge of factionalism.

Bukharin made the mistake of assuming that Stalin's policy of socialism in one country implied support for the NEP.

All of the contenders for power underestimated Stalin, because of:

- his ability to blend into the background
- his willingness to take on what others saw as unimportant, bureaucratic tasks.

Stalin's political skills
Despite being shrewd, cunning and ruthless, Stalin succeeded in seeming pragmatic, moderate and reasonable throughout the power struggle:

- He changed his position and alliances to make his opponents appear as factionalists. This was a charge levied at both the left and right. Lenin's Ban on Factions was used effectively against Trotsky and the Left Opposition the United Opposition and Bukharin.
- He correctly gauged public and party opinion. Policies, such as socialism in one country, had broad support and appealed to Russian patriotism. His rejection of the NEP by 1928 resonated with popular party sentiment and the desire for radical change.

It is not enough to notice that rivals made mistakes. Stalin showed great political skill in correctly assessing what the party membership wanted. He understood the discontent first with War Communism and then with the NEP, and adapted his economic views accordingly. His opposition to world revolution was popular. He thus presented himself as the cautious guardian of party and national unity, painting others as destabilising and untrustworthy. The power struggle, 1924–9, had resulted in Stalin becoming more than just Secretary-General. He was now the *vozhd*, or 'leader'.

Background issues to government policy
The key issues and contentious debates over government policy all favoured Stalin. Senior party figures, together with the general population, had little appetite for Trotsky's idea of world revolution. Socialism in one country seemed more moderate and appealed to ingrained Russian nationalism and pride. Similarly, Stalin's sharp change of direction over the NEP echoed the misgivings in the party over Lenin's policy.

The growing disillusionment with the NEP was even more apparent when the policy failed to deliver the promised economic growth after 1927. Stalin's policy of rapid industrialisation, coupled with the collectivisation of agriculture, therefore had the support of the majority within the party.

He has made concessions to us so that he can cut our throats [later].

Kamenev

Examiners' notes
If an exam question asks you to assess the reason for Stalin's victory in the leadership struggle, you should consider:

- Personality: what tactics were used and what mistakes were made by each rival?
- Positions: what posts did each candidate hold and what advantages or disadvantages did each position bring?
- Powerbase: what groups were each candidate's supporters and admirers?
- Background: what important political, economic and social decisions were being made during the struggle?

Examiners' notes

Exam questions will require you to understand the reasons driving change, and the connections between the reform of agriculture and changes in industry.

Essential notes

The most common type of collective farm was called a *kolkhoz*. Other types of collective farms included the *soukhoz*, in which everything was state property and the peasants were paid wages, and the *toz*, in which only land and labour were common.

Essential notes

Land had been nationalised in 1917, but livestock, tools and machinery were collectively owned by the peasants. In addition, each household was allotted one acre and some animals for family needs.

Essential notes

In a command economy, market forces do not drive business as they do in capitalism. Instead, the government decides which goods are produced, in what quantities, how they are distributed, what prices are charged and how much people are paid.

The collectivisation of agriculture

Historically, most Russian peasants had worked land which they rented from the village council, or *obshchina*. According to historian Orlando Figes, the left in Tsarist times had thought these village councils and the sharing of land showed that the peasants were naturally socialist.

Other peasants worked on large estates owned by the nobility. After the revolution, the Bolsheviks had ordered the break-up of large estates, sharing land out in small peasant farms. This had been popular in the countryside, but had reduced agricultural efficiency. Many people just grew what they needed to eat but the government needed to feed the proletariat in the cities, and also to export produce to earn money. By the second half of the 1920s, exports and imports were down to about a third of what they had been less than 15 years earlier, before the First World War.

Modernisation and collectivisation

The principal aim of Stalin's economic policies in the late 1920s was rapid modernisation. This was achieved in two ways:

- collectivisation
- industrialisation.

The collectivisation of agriculture was used to fund industrialisation: the reform was intended to create large, efficient and productive farms. As part of this process the Soviet state took over direct management, becoming a command economy.

Reasons for collectivisation

Ideology

An industrialised society with a substantial urban proletariat would conform more to Marxist theories of a socialist society than one in which most of the population were peasants and agriculture vastly outweighed industry in the economy. This would replace the more capitalist NEP. The Bolsheviks' initial assumption was that poor and landless peasants would form a natural alliance with the urban proletariat. In fact they allied with richer peasants, because the *obshchina* had been a unifying influence.

Collectivise then industrialise

In order to industrialise, the authorities needed to move workers from the countryside to towns and cities for the new factories. However, this created a renewed risk of famine. How would farms grow more food with fewer labourers? Where was the food going to come from for all these workers in the towns and cities?

Stalin decided that in order to achieve industrialisation, the land and the peasants had to be more ruthlessly exploited. Collectivisation would achieve this:

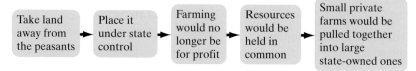

Stalin's plan for collectivisation

The expectation was that larger farms would be more efficient. Farm machinery such as tractors would be provided by the state for each large collective farm in a way that would not be possible given countless small private peasant farms. The newly mechanised, larger-scale agriculture would require fewer peasants to work the land, thus releasing labour for industry.

Power struggle
The policy of collectivisation was an integral part of Stalin's campaign against the right during the last stages of the power struggle. Implementing the policy would allow Stalin to stamp his authority on the party.

Pragmatism
Many in the Soviet leadership believed that the Soviet Union was about to be attacked by the capitalist West, as it had been in the civil war. Stalin knew that the USSR needed more industry to produce the military hardware necessary to defend itself. In addition, the economy needed further industrialisation to produce the manufactured goods needed by its population.

Grain Procurement Crisis
There were particularly poor harvests from 1927–9, and this was matched by prices rising as demand outstripped supply. This in turn increased the peasants' reluctance to hand over so valuable a commodity, just at a time when it was scarcest. This created the Grain Procurement Crises of 1927–8 and 1928–9, as many peasants preferred to store produce instead of handing a proportion over to government agents. State demands and peasant desires collided fatally. With this as the background, Stalin undertook a two-week tour of Siberia in January 1928, during which he revised his opinion of the NEP and moved to coercion as the method to be used.

In 1928, poorer peasants were encouraged to denounce richer ones for hoarding grain. Party officials would then take the grain from the richer peasants, who would be arrested and exiled or executed.

Forcible procurement produced the required amount of grain for the state, despite occurring at a time of poor harvests. Stalin ordered this Ural-Siberian Method to be adopted nationally to solve some of the problems of grain supply.

Although the grain harvest was better in 1929, many peasants still resisted and refused to sell their grain. In the cities, workers were on the brink of starvation. Stalin invented a scapegoat in the *kulaks*, a class of rich peasants he accused of hoarding their grain. The crisis saw the demise of the NEP, precipitating the new policy of collectivisation.

Essential notes
The Grain Procurement Crisis acted as a spur for the end of the NEP and the introduction of collectivisation. Stalin used the crisis to demonstrate the failure of the NEP.

Examiners' notes
There are a lot of motives, methods and consequences to keep track of in the question of collectivisation. When revising, remember three headings: fund industrialisation, staff factories, feed towns.

Continued on the next two pages

> The way out is to turn the small and scattered peasant farms into large united farms ... to introduce collective cultivation of the soil on the basis of a new and higher technique ... to unite the small and dwarf peasant farms gradually but surely, not by pressure, but by example and persuasion, into large farms based on common, cooperative collective cultivation of the soil with the use of agricultural machines and tractors and scientific methods of intensive agriculture.
>
> Stalin, 1927, on the purposes of collectivisation

Examiners' notes

When answering questions about the impact of collectivisation, you must be careful to understand the range of answer expected. Collectivisation affected not only agriculture and the peasantry, but also urbanisation and industrialisation.

The process of collectivisation

Collectivisation took place in stages. Stalin was initially cautious. At the 15th Congress of the Russian Communist Party (1927), Stalin had presented collectivisation as voluntary. However, the Grain Procurement Crisis of 1928–9, and the experience in the Urals and Siberia, changed his approach. In 1929, at the beginning of the process, less than 5 per cent of peasants lived and worked on state-owned farms. In January 1930, Stalin demanded that a quarter of the areas where grain was grown should be collectivised by the end of the year. By February 1930, Soviet officials heralded the success of collectivisation, with 50 per cent of all peasant households collectivised.

Emergency measures

Stalin's response to the supply crisis was to increase the central control of the state over the economy, 1928–9:

- meat, bread and other basic foodstuffs were rationed

- meat and grain were requisitioned.

There were also changes made to the Criminal Code:

- Article 107: grain hoarding was made illegal

- Article 61: Communist Party and the OGPU were given power to deport people to labour camps.

Dekulakisation

In December 1929, Stalin gave orders for the 'liquidation of the *kulaks* as a class'. The Soviet authorities worked with the Secret Police and anti-*kulak* squads, sent to the countryside to terrorise the peasants. They confiscated land and belongings, arrested entire families, and often sent the victims to labour camps.

The ideological theory was that *kulaks* were wealthy. In fact, poor as well as prosperous families were at risk of persecution.

The Twenty-five-thousanders

It was decided by the Central Committee of the Communist Party to mobilise 25 000 Communist Party militants and send them to rural areas to supervise the creation of collective farms. With anti-*kulak* zeal, these activists sometimes banished entire families and villages to labour camps. The murderous campaign was a warning to others of the consequences of resisting the state.

The impact of peasant resistance

Ownership of the land had been the longstanding peasant demand. Collectivisation was met with hostility and, in some cases, resistance:

- 30 000 arson attacks reported in the first year of collectivisation

- increase in organised protests: from 172 to 229 in 1929–30

- more than a quarter of all cattle, pigs and sheep destroyed by February 1929 as peasants refuse to hand them to the state
- peasants hoarded or destroyed grain, refusing to fill quotas
- farm machinery destroyed.

Stalin wrote an article in *Pravda* ('Dizzy with Success') in March 1930 stating that party officials may have been overzealous in enforcing collectivisation. This change of approach was intended to prevent:

- social unrest from getting out of control
- policy of industrialisation being derailed
- Stalin's control of the party and the country being called into question.

The change of approach was tactical and temporary. Once the harvests had been gathered in, Stalin restarted his collectivisation campaign with renewed vigour and brutality.

Social impact

The human cost of collectivisation was high. The government's policy of seizing grain continued, quite ignoring the fall in production. As a result, rural areas found themselves deprived of food. In Ukraine, the largest grain-producing region in the Soviet Union, the farms were expected to deliver increased grain quotas in 1931 and 1932. Historian Robert Conquest argues that Ukraine suffered especially harsh treatment as a warning to the rest of the USSR.

Large numbers of party activists, reinforced by the Secret Police, were recruited to crush peasant resistance. They searched houses, barns and fields to find grain that had been hidden by peasants. The actions of these 'requisitioning gangs' were legitimised by Stalin's draconian Seven-Eighths Law. This threatened anyone withholding property belonging to the state (including agricultural produce) with prison or execution.

In the first months of 1932, parts of Ukraine were experiencing a famine. During 1932–4 famine spread to other parts of the Soviet Union. The north Caucasus was badly affected. Kazakhstan lost a quarter of its population and 90 per cent of its livestock. Conquest argues that 7 million people died in this famine. This was a direct result of Stalin's collectivisation policy, so some historians have called it an artificial or man-made famine.

Human tragedy

An estimated 10 million people were exiled, ending up in prison camps or as slave labourers on one of Stalin's great industrialisation projects. Of these, it is estimated that 2 to 3 million died.

Essential notes

Agricultural productivity fell and the country grew less food. It was not until 1935 that grain production returned to 1928 levels. The peasants' private plots of land were a lifeline for many communities at this time. By 1937, these plots yielded over half of all vegetables and fruit, and nearly three-quarters of meat and milk.

Essential notes

The Seven-Eighths Law protected *kolkhoz* workers and state property on *kolkhozes*. The law banned both theft and gleaning. Punishments included shooting and ten years in a labour camp. It was named after the date it was passed, 7 August 1932, written 7/8/1932. Estimates are that nearly 200 000 people were sent to labour camps and more than 10 000 were executed under this law.

Essential notes

In this and other cases, precise figures are difficult to obtain. The Soviet authorities refused to acknowledge the existence of the famine, the Central Statistical Bureau withheld data and individual officials falsified statistics.

The economic and political impact of collectivisation

Impact on economy

Economic and social successes

Stalin needed agricultural reform to support his programme of industrialisation. This was achieved. Between 1928 and 1935, the amount of grain procured more than doubled, though production remained stubbornly lower than it had been in Tsarist times before the First World War.

Collectivisation precipitated mass migration from the countryside to the cities, which accelerated urbanisation. This relieved the economic pressure on the land, and provided a workforce for industrialisation. By 1939, 19 million people had left the countryside for the towns and cities to escape the famine and find work. While this is what Stalin had intended, it left cities at risk of being inundated by economic migrants. Internal passports were introduced to control the movement of people and to prevent the cities from being overwhelmed by starving peasants.

Economic and social failures

The grain harvest dropped dramatically in the early 1930s and did not recover until the latter half of the decade. Even after that recovery the performance of the agricultural economy under Stalin remained worse than in the last years of Tsarist Russia:

- 1913: 80 million tonnes
- 1928: nearly 11 million tonnes of grain produced
- 1933: nearly 23 million tonnes
- 1935: 75 million tonnes

Reliable figures are hard to come by, but historians agree that by 1935 the number of livestock, such as cattle, pigs, sheep and goats, was about half that of 1928. That affected meat production, but the lack of draught animals – horses, oxen and donkeys – also meant there were not enough animals to pull ploughs and carts, which affected arable farming.

These figures were compounded by the lack of expertise in the countryside. This was the result of two key problems:

- *Dekulakisation* stripped village communities of the most able and knowledgeable farmers.
- Officials sent to implement collectivisation were party loyalists, not agricultural experts.

Without the demands of their own farms and livestock, the peasants lost a key incentive for working. Collective farms did not motivate individual initiative and long hours. In addition, agricultural workers did not have the same care for communally owned livestock and machinery as they had for something they had bought themselves.

The use of force and terror meant that grain procurement remained high even when harvests were poor and grain production low. The state could thus continue to feed its growing industrial workforce in the cities and even

Examiners' notes

When evaluating the extent to which collectivisation was a *success*, you must consider more than the human costs. Remember to use Stalin's aims as a basis for your judgement. What did he hope to achieve through his policy of collectivisation? To what extent did he achieve this?

Essential notes

Grain procurement continued even during times of famine. However, the Soviet authorities discontinued grain exports in 1933 at the end of the First Five-Year Plan.

Essential notes

The Secret Police, now known as the OGPU, organised the *dekulakisation* of the countryside. The OGPU also supervised the internal passport system. Not only could they monitor the movement of the peasants to the cities, they could also check the movements of suspected political opposition.

sell grain abroad to fund Stalin's industrialisation drive during the First Five-Year Plan. While it meant that towns were fed even in times of famine, grain procurement could deprive the countryside, leading to famine.

Political successes

The state's control of the countryside was strengthened. Collectivisation was driven through and with every year the proportion of collectivised land rose:

- 1928: 2.7%
- 1934: 71.4%
- 1936: 89.6%
- 1941: 98%

Collectivisation destroyed the peasantry as a political force, leaving them no longer able to oppose government policy.

The process had also made the enforcement role of the Secret Police central to the Soviet state. There were now agents in every part of the countryside as there were in the towns. This meant that Stalin's authority and the authority of the party in the countryside were enforced by the Secret Police.

Collectivisation shored up Stalin's credentials as a socialist leader. Market forces no longer dominated agriculture. Peasants no longer refused to sell their grain, denying the urban proletariat a steady supply of food.

Success or failure?

In 1927 Stalin had declared that the USSR needed to collectivise its agriculture.

This was certainly achieved:

- 1928: 97.3% agricultural land was privately farmed
- 1941: 98% agricultural land was collectivised.

However, two things did not increase: the total amount produced and the surplus available for sale; peasants held on to more of the food they grew.

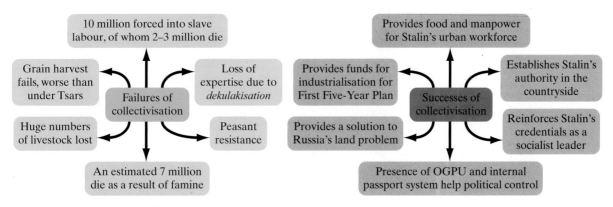

Collectivisation – success or failure?

The First Five-Year Plan

Gosplan and the Five-Year Plans

The Five-Year Plans were central to Stalin's efforts to industrialise the USSR. The typical model of a managed economy, these plans set the targets and quotas that each industry was expected to meet. These were enshrined in law: if not achieved, managers and workers could be punished; if met or surpassed, there were rewards.

Gosplan, the State Planning Commission, had been established in 1921:

- it coordinated the Five-Year Plans
- it determined the resources required for each industry
- it set the targets for each industry
- it competed with *Vesenkha* (Supreme Economic Council) for influence.

Heading the process was the Commissar for Heavy Industry.

Priorities of the First Five-Year Plan

The First Five-Year Plan (1928–33) was significant for its ever-increasing targets. The original targets for the plan were revised upwards and were wholly unrealistic. Stalin wanted his plans for rapid industrialisation to put the USSR on a war footing. Thus the emphasis of the First Five-Year Plan was on heavy industry – coal, oil, steel, electricity and cement.

Successes of the First Five-Year Plan

In the First Five-Year Plan, oil production actually exceeded the targets set. The production of electricity, coal and iron missed their targets but still increased massively. The production of machine tools, electric motors, locomotives and turbines increased as a result of the advancements in engineering industries and the creation of new factories, such as tractor factories in Stalingrad. The production of heavy machinery was important in meeting the needs of both collectivisation and the Five-Year Plans.

Enormous industrial works and even whole cities were created in inhospitable, but mineral-rich, areas. The existing coal industry in the Kuznetsk Basin (in Siberia) and Donbas (in Ukraine) grew. Serviced by the Trans-Siberian Railway, by 1932 Kuznetsk was producing 7.544 million tonnes of low sulphur, energy-efficient coal.

Production of	1928	1933
Electricity	5 billion kWh	16.4 billion kWh
Coal	35.5 million tonnes	76.3 million tonnes
Pig-iron	3.3 million tonnes	7.1 million tonnes
Rolled steel	3.4 million tonnes	5.1 million tonnes
Quality steel	0.09 million tonnes	0.89 million tonnes
Metal cutting tools	2000	21 000
Tractors	18 000	79 900

The First Five-Year Plan

Failures of the First Five-Year Plan

Perhaps one of the most notable characteristics of the First Five-Year Plan was the lack of attention given to improving the standard of living of Soviet citizens.

Consumer industries progressed very little or even worsened. The production of woollen textiles, for example, declined during this period from 101 million metres in 1928 to 86 million metres in 1933. The emphasis on heavy industries meant that consumer goods were often in short supply – shops were empty and many household goods were almost impossible to obtain. Stalin expected that the workers would make sacrifices in order to help the Soviet Union industrialise.

The workforce consisted mostly of unskilled, illiterate peasants who had recently left the collectivised countryside. A shortage of skilled, experienced workers meant that production targets were often not met and the quality of goods produced was unreliable. Furthermore, the targets set were for quantity, not quality: the volume of output was what mattered.

... unrealistic and the consequences of failure were harsh.
... er of their
... emic as frightened
..., would try to bribe their

... rand economic schemes.
... ntomania'.

... his. In 1929, it was still an
... izens on the east side of
... mining and industrial city
... e 250 000 volunteer
... alling conditions to mine
... huts or wooden shacks
... withstood only a couple of
... did double shifts, believing

Essential notes

The gigantomania approach encouraged ambitious plans that the system was unable to carry through. Attempts to meet unrealistic targets created a demand for slave labour. Thus the policies of oppression, industrialisation and modernisation went hand in hand.

Dnieper in Ukraine supported the largest hydroelectric plant in Europe and provided all the energy needed for industry in the region.

The White Sea Canal, opened in 1933, connected the White and Baltic Seas, to improve trade access to the West. Built by slave labour from the *gulag* camps, as many as 100 000 people may have died in its construction.

Map showing major industrial centres in the USSR, 1930s

31

The Second Five-Year Plan

During the First Five-Year Plan, Western powers began to suffer from the Great Depression. This began in the USA in 1929 and during the 1930s spread throughout the world. The downturn in trade and economic slowdown spread to all industrialised and then even pre-industrialised countries, and formed the background particularly to the Second Five-Year Plan. The Second Five-Year Plan (1933–7) followed the same path as the First. However, targets were more achievable and efforts were made to learn from previous mistakes. Initially there was some emphasis on consumer goods. However, by the end of the Second Five-Year Plan, the focus on consumer goods was replaced by a stress on heavy industry to help with rearmament in response to growing German militarism.

	1933	1934	1935	1936	1937
Total budget (millions of roubles)	42 080	55 444	73 571	92 480	106 238
Defence	1421	5019	8186	14 883	17 481
% of total	3.4	9.1	11.1	16.1	16.5

(From Alec Nove, *An Economic History of the USSR*, 1984, pages 228–9)

Defence expenditure in the Second Five-Year Plan

Nevertheless, new industries such as chemical processing developed, as did the communications and transport industries, especially the railways.

Successes of the Second Five-Year Plan

Many of the schemes started in the First Five-Year Plan were completed, increasing industrial growth. As a consequence, during 1934–6 the Soviet Union experienced three years of relative economic prosperity.

Heavy industries profited from the completed projects of the First Five-Year Plan. For example, hydroelectric plants depending on the Dnieprostroi Dam or the Svir'-Neva Project, which powered Leningrad, generated vast amounts of electricity.

Transport, such as railways, speedily developed in response to the growing economic need for an advanced communication network. The country's first underground railway system opened in 1935 in Moscow.

Chemical industries developed quickly. By 1937, the Soviet Union produced 3.24 tonnes of fertiliser for agriculture. The economies of cities such as Kalinin and Redkino benefited from the advances in the chemical industry, as their populations expanded to meet employment opportunities.

Metallurgical industries expanded, spurred on by the discovery of new natural resources in remote areas. Copper, mercury, manganese, platinum and chromium were mined in the Urals; lead and zinc were mined in Siberia.

	1932 (actual)	1937 (plan)	1937 (actual)
National income (million roubles)	45 500	100 200	96 300
Gross industrial production (million roubles)	43 300	92 712	95 500

(From Alec Nove, *An Economic History of the USSR*, page 226)

Achievements of the Second Five-Year Plan

Stakhanovism

The First Five-Year Plan exposed the inadequacy of the poorly trained, inexperienced and ill-disciplined Soviet workforce. The government launched a new propaganda drive, creating the image of an intrepid Soviet worker capable of superhuman efforts.

On the morning of 30 August 1935, Alexei Stakhanov, a coalminer, began work. In less than six hours he had mined almost 14 times more coal than was normally produced in a single shift. He was lauded for his achievement. He received 200 roubles, a spacious apartment and a holiday at a resort. He gave his name to a new movement: Stakhanovism. Workers across the USSR were asked to emulate his example. The propaganda did not mention that his achievement had been stage-managed by a local party boss. Stakhanov had been set up with the best-available equipment and supported by a team in a way that miners rarely were.

The Stakhanovite movement extended to other industries in the Soviet Union. The Soviet authorities claimed that the Stakhanovite movement had caused a significant increase in labour productivity, and awarded medals to successful workers as part of the propaganda drive. The achievements of individuals were used to justify the raising of quotas, sometimes by as much as 50 per cent.

Failures of the Second Five-Year Plan

Oil production advanced only modestly throughout the Second Five-Year Plan. In 1933 the production of crude oil was 21.5 million tonnes, and by 1937 this rose to 28.5 million tonnes. By the end of 1937, the USSR experienced a fuel crisis.

Although there was some effort made to improve consumer industries, for example in footwear and food processing, this section of the economy was still considered less important than heavy industry. As a result, shortages remained a daily feature of Soviet life, which resulted in endless queuing to buy food, clothing and household goods. Soviet statisticians recorded a rise of 80 per cent in the prices of bread and eggs.

The rush to the towns created by collectivisation in the countryside was not matched by an adequate building programme. As a result, many or perhaps most industrial workers lived in squalid, overcrowded conditions.

Examiners' notes

Questions on the success of the Five-Year Plans recur frequently. If answering one, you are likely to need to analyse what was achieved. However, in addition to reporting on whether key targets were met, you might consider that there is a difference between failure to produce goods in sufficient quantity or to a sufficient quality, and some of the quality-of-life failures. Also, were these shortfalls failures or actually planned outcomes?

Essential notes

Increased production created a massive rise in the demand for energy, which the country's oil industry struggled to meet. This is an example of the difficulties faced by Soviet planners.

Essential notes

For the British, the Second World War began in 1939. For the Czechs it began in 1938 when Czechoslovakia was invaded by Germany. For the Soviets, what the USSR government called the Great Patriotic War began with Hitler's Operation Barbarossa, when German forces invaded the USSR in 1941.

The Third Five-Year Plan

Context

International background

The Third Five-Year Plan (1938–41) was cut short after just three and a half years by the German invasion of the Soviet Union in June 1941. The main emphasis of the Third Five-Year Plan was the preparation for war.

As war approached, more resources were put into developing armaments, as well as constructing additional military factories east of the Ural Mountains. This was a continuation of the final phase of the Second Five-Year Plan. By 1940, over 30 per cent of government finances went to the military and consumer industry was once again a low priority. As in the First Five-Year Plan, emphasis was placed on quantity rather than quality.

Domestic background

The Third Five-Year Plan coincided with the purges of what historian Robert Conquest has called the 'Great Terror'. Purges deprived workplaces of managers and skilled workers. It left those who remained too terrified to make decisions. The system of planning was thrown into chaos.

Successes of the Third Five-Year Plan

Heavy industry continued to expand as an estimated 4200 million roubles went to defence spending. Annual aircraft production during the First Five-Year Plan was 860. In the approach to war, 1938–40, this figure rose to 8805. There were similar increases in tank numbers: 740 in 1930–1; 2672 by 1938–40.

Twenty-four new explosives factories and six extra aircraft factories were built. By June 1941, the Soviet Union was numerically superior to Germany in weaponry. It possessed over 15 000 tanks and nearly 12 000 aircraft.

Production in related areas rose too: by 1940 the USSR was producing 165.9 million tonnes of coal.

Failures of the Third Five-Year Plan

There was a shortage of materials and resources for many factories, leading to delays in production.

Steel production was stagnant. In 1937 the production of rolled steel was 13 million tonnes. By 1940 it had only risen to 13.1 million tonnes. Quality steel only rose from 2.39 million tonnes in 1937 to 2.79 million tonnes by 1940. Industries central to war (such as steel-producing factories, aircraft industries) were located in the west, vulnerable to attack.

Oil production, as in the Second Five-Year Plan, remained modest. The USSR produced only 31.1 million tonnes of crude oil in 1940, not even 3 million tonnes more than in 1937.

Consumer industries were again of secondary importance. The standard of living for most Soviet citizens stayed low. The needs of Soviet workers remained subordinate to the needs of industry and the state.

The USSR's mineral reserves remained underdeveloped.

Finally, the usual quota-driven emphasis on quantity over quality mean that many of the weapons would prove technically inferior.

Essential notes

Issues of quality became significant with the 1941 German invasion. Many Soviet weapons proved technically inferior to those of the invader when put to the test (see pages 62–63).

Five-Year Plans 1928–41

First Five-Year Plan	Second Five-Year Plan		Third Five-Year Plan
• Heavy industry • Gigantomania • Unrealistic targets	• Heavy industry • Transport and communications • Consumer industry	• The Great Depression • Stakhanovism • Defence	• Heavy industry • Defence • The Great Patriotic War

The first three Five-Year Plans: a summary

Successes and failures

During the period from 1928 to 1941, the first three Five-Year Plans had changed the Soviet Union. However, a critic could characterise this change as being from an inefficient agrarian economy to an inefficient industrialised economy.

The population of the USSR increased from 147 million in 1926 to 170 million at the outbreak of hostilities with Germany. In 1926, 18 per cent of the population lived in the cities; by 1939, a third of the Soviet people lived in a major industrial conurbation.

Industrialisation had been achieved at vast cost to the Soviet people. We shall never know how many hundreds of thousands of slave labourers died in the gigantomania projects. We do know that the deaths from the famines created or worsened by collectivisation run into millions.

We also know that the ordinary workers suffered hard labour, persistent shortages of basic goods, overcrowded housing and a low standard of living.

The Five-Year Plans, despite intermittently reassessed priorities, continually focused on heavy industry and armaments. Even though industrial growth was high (the authorities claimed it was around 12 per cent per annum), the Soviet economy was imbalanced and inefficient. Soviet claims and statistics about the successes of the Five-Year Plans were not credible; they were embelished by propaganda, managers and party officials.

Examiners' notes

You should be able to identify the changing priorities and emphases of the Five-Year Plans. This will help you answer questions about the extent to which Stalin's aims or policies changed.

Essential notes

Stalin and the Soviet government had altered the Soviet Union. They had done so with the labour of:

- thousands of idealistic volunteers
- tens of thousands of unjustly imprisoned slave labourers
- millions of poorly trained workers driven from peasant agriculture by collectivisation.

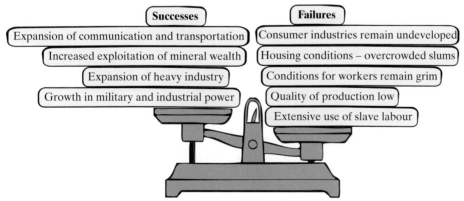

Successes	Failures
Expansion of communication and transportation	Consumer industries remain undeveloped
Increased exploitation of mineral wealth	Housing conditions – overcrowded slums
Expansion of heavy industry	Conditions for workers remain grim
Growth in military and industrial power	Quality of production low
	Extensive use of slave labour

How far had the Five-Year Plans and industrialisation changed the USSR, 1928–41?

Stalin's social policies

Lenin's legacy

The Bolsheviks came to power with the express purpose of creating a society free from both economic exploitation and social exploitation. Influenced by Marx's co-author Friedrich Engels, the Communist Party believed that under capitalism women had been subjugated and abused. In the years after 1917, the government led by Lenin:

- made divorce available upon the request of either husband or wife

- legalised abortion on demand

- promised childcare, kindergartens and crèches for working women

- provided communal canteens and laundries to free women from their domestic burdens.

Sexual relationships between people who were not married, called at the time 'free love', became seemingly more socially acceptable.

In 1919, the *Zhenotdel* was established to ensure women's social equality and to encourage women to play a more active role in the political and economic life of the country.

There was ambivalence among the communist leadership from the beginning. Lenin himself began to have doubts over the efficacy of the radical social policies; Stalin proved to be a social conservative.

Women, the family, marriage and divorce under Stalin

In 1930 Stalin declared that the aims of the *Zhenotdel* had been accomplished and the organisation was abolished. He gradually changed official Soviet policy – this was known as the 'Great Retreat'. In the 1936 Stalin Constitution, women's equality with men was enshrined in the constitution. Despite this, Stalin's policies abandoned the Bolshevik social experiment and reverted to traditional attitudes towards women, the family, divorce and abortion.

Women and children

Collectivisation and industrialisation had led to a dramatic decline in the birth rate in the 1930s.

In an effort to reverse this trend, the Communist Party offered rewards to mothers of large families. Mothers with seven children received an annual sum of 2000 roubles for five years; mothers with 11 children received 5000 roubles. Medals were also awarded.

In 1936 abortion was prohibited in all but a handful of cases where the woman's life was in danger. These measures changed the number of live births (in a population of more than 100 million) from 2.923 million in 1934 to 3.814 million in 1940.

Family life, marriage and divorce

Stalin declared that the family was the cornerstone of Soviet society and the Soviet government stressed the importance of marriage. Party

Essential notes

The *Zhenotdel* was the Women's Section of the Central Committee of the Communist Party.

Essential notes

Stalin called the 1936 Stalin Constitution 'the most democratic in the world'. It guaranteed civil liberties and equality, including freedom of speech and assembly, to all Soviet citizens regardless of social origin or gender. Some historians consider the Constitution to have been little more than a propaganda document.

members who were married were given superior housing and a holiday home. By 1937, 91 per cent of men and 82 per cent of women between the ages of 30 and 39 were married. Male party members were expected to be as devoted to their wives and family as they were to the party and in theory could be expelled if they had extramarital affairs.

Stalin reversed the lenient divorce laws of the 1920s, making divorce more difficult. There was a substantial fee for the divorce to proceed. Additionally, divorced men were expected to pay a considerable proportion of their monthly salary in child support.

In 1934, a decree held parents criminally responsible for the actions of their children. This made the family part of the state's system of social discipline.

Women and work

Stalin's economic policies compelled him to adopt a contradictory policy towards women and work. A major change affecting women was the expansion of the female labour force, which was driven by the regime's industrialisation programme. They joined the workforce in increasing numbers because of the requirements of the Five-Year Plans.

In 1931, Stalin launched a recruitment drive for an additional 1.6 million women. The number of female workers rose from 3 million in 1928, at the start of the First Five-Year Plan, to 13 million in 1940.

Most women remained employed in traditional sectors, such as the public services or light industry, such as textiles. During the Third Five-Year Plan women increasingly took up jobs in heavy industry:

- 1930: women were 28 per cent of the *total* industry workforce
- 1939: women were 39 per cent of the *total* industry workforce
- 1940: women were 43 per cent of *heavy* industry workforce

Women were paid less than men even if they were doing the same job, receiving between 60–65 per cent of a man's salary.

In agriculture, the massive migration to the towns and cities had been dominated by men. This left women as a majority of the agricultural workforce. By 1939, 20 million women made up 58 per cent of the farming workforce. Even here tasks were often gender specific. While men operated mechanical equipment, manual labour was left to women.

While the increasing number of women in the workplace may seem a progressive change, it increased the pressure on them. Even when they went out to work, they remained responsible for domestic chores.

Was there progress for women?

After the revolution, policies on women and the family had been driven by a confident enthusiasm for change: the Bolsheviks were setting out to create a new kind of society. Stalin reversed many of the changes because his interconnected priorities – collectivisation, industrialisation, defence – demanded social stability and social discipline, and he identified the family as a key means of achieving this.

Examiners' notes

Exam questions may focus not just on Soviet social policies towards women, the family and divorce between 1928 and 1941, but also on the degree of change.

Education

Soviet education in 1924

When they came to power, Lenin and the Bolsheviks had rejected anything that they considered to be 'bourgeois' or which retained the attitudes of the Tsarist society that had been overthrown in the revolution. By 1924, reform had undermined much in traditional education. Among the things that had been criticised were textbooks, exams and the authority of teachers.

Education under Stalin

Stalin's educational policy in the 1930s had two specific aims, both created the needs of his social and economic policies:

- create a skilled workforce
- create a governable society.

Education was essential to creating a modern industrial state. To be productive, the workforce must possess at least basic literacy and numeracy skills. Industrialisation could not move forward without skilled workers. The First Five-Year Plan was adversely affected by the fact that so much of the workforce was uneducated and untrained. Such a workforce had been all very well for a Tsarist government that assumed most people would largely go on doing what they and their parents had always done. But the Soviet government had timetabled industrialisation and collectivisation: such radical changes demanded the workers learn to do new things and for that they needed education and training.

The years of wars and revolution had left a legacy of rebelliousness. Stalin needed a governable society of workers who would act with unquestioning obedience to the authority of the Communist Party – and of Stalin personally. Formal, academic education was made a priority, along with the recognition of the need for discipline and order. This would instil in the young skills and values needed in the workplace and in a one-party state. Organisations like the *Komsomol* instructed children to respect their parents and those in authority.

Thus what education could offer dovetailed with what the Five-Year Plans demanded.

From 1930, primary education was compulsory

Key features of Stalin's education system

From 1930, primary education was compulsory. This was further developed to guarantee every child ten years' mandatory schooling. From 1935, children all learned reading, writing, mathematics, science, history, geography, Russian and communist ideology. History is a relevant example of the changes in the nature of education under Stalin. In the early years of the Bolshevik government, history was taught in terms of the exploitation of one class by another. But under Stalin, every child would learn a sense of national pride.

Stalin reversed many of the innovations put in place by Lenin and the Bolsheviks:

- state-authorised textbooks were to be used
- homework, banned in the 1920s, was to be assigned regularly
- students would sit public examinations
- by the late 1930s, school uniforms were required
- fees were to be charged for the last three years of non-compulsory schooling
- scholarships were offered to the offspring of party and trade union members.

The Great Retreat

With the introduction of fees for schooling at ages 15–18 and scholarships for the children of party and trade-union members, the Soviet system now included private education. This is another startling example of what the Russian writer Nicholas S. Timasheff called the 'Great Retreat'. The government presented its arguments in a way that mingled pragmatism, patriotism and communism.

1. The first argument presented by the state was that Soviet society needed specialists, such as doctors, engineers and teachers, and this required an educational system capable of producing them.

2. The second argument was that the system was allowing the talented to be selected purely on the grounds of their ability; this was different from before the 1917 Revolution when what counted was the pupils' (and their parents') class.

The system, however, created an elite: some won scholarships and stayed on at school beyond 15; some went to university; and some joined the new professional, governing class.

Most workers and peasants did not have these opportunities. This process in turn meant that the newly developing educated elite owed their position to Stalin and had good reason therefore for being loyal to him personally.

Examiners' notes

Exam questions may look at the changing aims and values of the Stalinist period. You should note these changes to the educational system and consider their significance in that context.

Essential notes

Zinoviev coined the phrase 'Homo Sovieticus' to describe the new breed of 'Soviet Man' that such children might grow up to become.

Continued on the next two pages

Essential notes

Access to further and higher education was more accessible to the children of party members, but also taken up by some nationalities more than others. Russians, Ukrainians and Jews were the majority in universities; other ethnic groups were less well represented.

The results of Stalin's educational reforms

Date	Changes made
1933	18 million children in primary education (9 million in 1920)
1933	3.5 million children in secondary education (0.5 million in 1922)
1937	Census data for that year revealed a literacy rate of 75 per cent: 86 per cent for men and 65 per cent for women (adult literacy 25 per cent in 1917)
1939	In cities, schooling for children aged 8–14 had become the norm
1941	Total attendance at school reaches 35 million

The effect of Stalin's educational reforms

Universities

The Soviet Union's most esteemed institution of tertiary education was the Academy of Sciences, which incorporated 250 research organisations. Despite its name, it included arts, agriculture, medicine and management. In 1935 the government sought to control the Academy directly, ending any semblance of independent research. Thereafter, the Academy upheld Stalin's vision of socialism. In return for forfeiting their intellectual independence, scholars were rewarded with superior academic and social benefits.

The teaching of subjects such as history, literature and philosophy were all affected by state interference, with an insistence on a correct Marxist-Leninist approach being adopted in each case. For example, history was used to build up patriotism in the run up to war. Social sciences were unsurprisingly dominated by Marxist-Leninist assumptions about social class. However, the sciences were not immune from politicisation.

Lysenko affair

The pitfalls of the loss of independence by the Academy of Sciences show up in the Lysenko affair, which damaged the reputation of both Soviet agriculture and science.

Trofim Lysenko was an expert in agricultural science who developed an alleged 'super-crop' that could withstand cold, was resistant to disease and produced a harvest 16 times greater than normal crops. Lysenko was from a peasant family. His ideas went against accepted scientific research. Clearly there was a pragmatic imperative to increase yields from farms. To be able to do this without using fertilisers or minerals would be an economic bonus. To have this development come from a peasant's son (not a member of any university or academy) was a propaganda advantage. Stalin accepted Lysenko's ideas and in 1941 Lysenko was awarded the Stalin Prize. 'Lysenkoism' was accepted by almost no eminent scientist outside those countries dominated by the Soviet Union, yet it dominated scientific discussion in the USSR. It was only after Stalin's death that Lysenko was exposed as a fraud in his own country.

Trofim Lysenko examines wheat growing at a collective farm near Odessa, Ukraine

Successes and failures

To the extent that Stalin's educational policy was to create a trained workforce and an obedient society, it could be regarded as a success. But a healthy educational environment, like a healthy society, needs debate, and debate was not something Stalin allowed. The Lysenko scandal was only the best-known example of politics distorting scientific life. Many historians of science argue that the stifling of debate held back Soviet science, just as the intervention of the NKVD suffocated Soviet arts.

A further test of the educational reforms was the support they gave to the Five-Year Plans. Here again the conclusions are mixed. Soviet economic growth was impressive, even if the official statistics are treated with necessary caution:

- a trained and disciplined workforce was created

- targets were met

- strikes and disruption were reduced.

However, while the targets for quantities were being met, insufficient attention was being given to quality and many of the goods produced were of a low standard.

The origins of the Terror

Lenin's legacy

In 1918, Lenin reintroduced the institution of Secret Police, known as the *Cheka*, into Russian political life. Between 1918 and 1920, it is estimated the *Cheka* were responsible for the deaths of nearly 300 000 people. The Red Terror, which accompanied the civil war, was an escalation in the use of violence against political enemies. Those arrested were accused of being *kulaks* and counter-revolutionaries. Lenin famously sent a telegram demanding that officials publicly hang 'at least 100 notorious *kulaks* ... Execute the hostages.' As in the Stalinist purges of the 1930s, such labels really meant anyone who opposed the Bolsheviks.

Did Lenin lead to Stalin?

Historian Robert Conquest argues that Lenin introduced political terror into Soviet politics. According to this approach, Stalin merely intensified the violent tendency that was present in Bolshevik politics from the outset. However, you should note that there were significant differences:

- Terror under Lenin occurred when the Bolsheviks were trying to seize and then consolidate their power. The Stalinist purges of the 1930s occurred when the communist government was entrenched in power.

- Lenin himself turned against the indiscriminate use of terror.

- The scale of the Terror of the 1920s pales in comparison with the comprehensive nature of the purges of the 1930s.

- Lenin used terror against the political enemies of the Bolsheviks; Stalin used terror against his own rivals within the Communist Party.

Causes of the Terror

Stalin's personality

Historian Alan Bullock has argued that Stalin was paranoid about any perceived opposition to his leadership, believing there were plotters within the party seeking to depose him. He distrusted:

- Bukharin, Kamenev and Zinoviev: Bullock thinks that Stalin hated anyone who was his intellectual superior.

- Trotsky, who was excluded from party membership and went into exile; even then Stalin suspected he still had loyal followers inside the Soviet Union.

- Old Bolsheviks who knew the contents of Lenin's *Testament* and remembered Stalin from the days before he held power.

- Leaders of the powerful institutions over which Stalin exercised least control, the Army and the Secret Police.

According to this explanation, the purges of the 1930s were the result of Stalin's unstable personality. Some biographers add that Stalin was affected enormously by the suicide of his wife, Nadia, in 1932.

Ryutin Platform

In fact, Stalin really did have opponents within the Communist Party. In 1930, Martemyan Ryutin circulated a long policy document that was critical of Stalin. Known as the Ryutin Platform, it described Stalin as 'The evil genius of the revolution who, motivated by a personal desire for power and revenge, brought the revolution to the verge of ruin'. Ryutin was arrested; he and his supporters were expelled from the party but cleared of criminal intent and membership was later restored. In 1932, he urged Stalin's overthrow and was again arrested. It was not until a retrial in 1937 that Stalin was able to have him killed.

Congress of Victors

The 1934 17th Party Congress was intended to be a 'Congress of Victors', celebrating Stalin's economic successes and the Five-Year Plans. At the Congress, Sergei Kirov received more votes than Stalin in the election for the Central Committee. A group of Bolsheviks approached Kirov and asked if he would stand against Stalin for the post of Secretary-General, but he refused. Instead of being Secretary-General, Stalin was now given the title of Secretary of Equal Rank alongside Kirov. Stalin's position as leader was under threat.

The murder of Kirov

On 1 December 1934, Kirov was shot by Leonid Nikolayev. The fact that the murder occurred so soon after the 17th Party Congress has led to widespread suspicion that Stalin was behind it. Certainly Kirov's death was beneficial to Stalin, so if it was not carefully plotted, then it was certainly quickly seized upon and used. Within two hours of Kirov's murder, Stalin had issued the Decree against Terrorist Acts, which gave the NKVD unrestricted powers to hunt down enemies of the state. Supposed plotters of Kirov's murder were arrested and imprisoned or executed.

Essential

Historian Robert Conquest writes in *The Great Terror*: 'Ryutin saw, far more clearly than his seniors in the opposition, that there was no possibility of controlling Stalin. It was a question either of submission or of revolt.'

Essential notes

NKVD was the People's Commissariat for Internal Affairs – the Secret Police between 1934 and 1943.

How Stalin benefited from Kirov's death

Essential notes

The Russian word *chistka* or 'cleansings' was the expression given to the occasional purges of the Communist Party to remove members whom the leadership considered disadvantageous to the cause. Before Stalin this process was non-violent.

Essential notes

Genrikh Yagoda was head of the NKVD 1934–6. He oversaw the post-Kirov purges in Leningrad and the Trial of the 16, including Kamenev and Zinoviev. Historians see these events as marking the beginning of the Great Terror. Yagoda was himself to be arrested in the purges.

The purges of 1934–6

Stalin's first purge of the party followed the arrest of Ryutin, who was convicted and again expelled from membership. From 1933 to 1934, one million party activists, approximately a third of the membership, were accused of being 'Ryutinites'. They were expelled, and they and their families lost the privileges of party membership. This was largely a bloodless purge.

Intensification of the purges under Yagoda

Purge of the party after Kirov's death

In 1935, the purge of the party resumed after the assassination of Kirov. Yagoda, head of the Secret Police, was appointed to lead the investigation, which focused on prominent party members. Following Nikolayev's confession that he killed Kirov on the orders of Trotsky, Zinoviev and others, Stalin commanded all party branches to expose 'Trotskyites' in their membership or locality.

Following Kirov's murder, a letter went from the Central Committee to Communist Party branches informing them in secret that there was a counter-revolutionary plot involving leftist followers of the leaders of the United Opposition, which had formed in 1926. Expelled in 1929, Trotsky was abroad, but Zinoviev and Kamenev came to trial in 1936 in the first of the Moscow Show Trials.

The arrest, trial and execution of Old Bolsheviks such as Zinoviev and Kamenev showed that whatever their party position or revolutionary past, no one was secure:

- More than half the delegates at the 1934 Congress of Victors had been executed by 1937.
- More than two thirds of the 1934 Central Committee died during the purges.

Show Trial of Zinoviev and Kamenev

Beginning in Leningrad, the purge spread across the country. Zinoviev and Kamenev were arrested, and they and 14 others were put on trial in 1936 in what is popularly known as the 'Trial of the 16'. All 16 were charged with Kirov's murder, as well as conspiracy to sabotage the Five-Year Plans. All confessed to the charges and all were shot. This was the First Moscow Show Trial, with the outcome a foregone conclusion. The trials were held not to discover guilt but to enforce Stalin's authority over the party.

Mechanisms of control during the purges

Control over the party machine

The post-Kirov purges allowed Stalin to tighten his grip on the party by filling key positions with his followers. These appointments left Stalin in control of every aspect of government and bureaucracy.

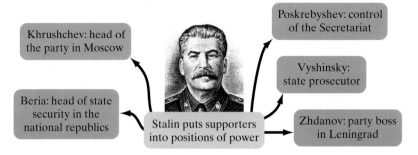

How Stalin controlled the party through his apointees

Stalin's supporters

Many of the appointees had come into the party in the 'Stalin Enrolment' of the early 1930s. These new members knew that their membership of the party – and all the benefits of that membership – depended on Stalin, so they were the more likely to support and enforce his decisions. In addition, purges created job vacancies. Those ambitious for promotion were all the more willing to participate in the purging of Stalin's opponents and supposed opponents within the party. Never again would there be a conference at which Stalin's leadership was challenged or questioned as at the 1934 17th Party Congress.

Discontent and the purges

The upheaval caused by both collectivisation and the Five-Year Plans, and later the downturn in the economy in 1937, had badly affected many ordinary people's lives. In the pursuit of Ryutinites, Trotskyites and others, Stalin and his supporters scapegoated individuals and groups. The deficiencies in the economic policy were thus not the responsibility of incompetent managers, nor an untrained workforce, nor corrupt officials. Propaganda alleged all to be the fault of 'wreckers' or 'industrial saboteurs' who were alleged to be in plots directed by Trotsky, Zinoviev and Kamenev.

Centralising law enforcement

Stalin brought all major law enforcement agencies under central control by 1934. The police, the Secret Police, and the different forces that guarded the borders and labour camps, were put under the control of the NKVD, which in turn was directly answerable to Stalin. The legal system was further politicised, with so-called 'serious' crimes taken out of the justice system and put in the hands of a military court. These crimes were political ones and the accused had no real chance of proving their innocence.

Essential notes

The resultant promotion opportunities brought economic benefits to bystanders that gave them a reason to support or at least ignore injustice and terror. The government too derived an economic benefit, as the purges sent slave labour to work on the major construction projects such as the Volga Canal, or dangerous work such as the Vorkuta labour camp's coalmines in northern Siberia.

Examiners' notes

Exam questions on the purges might ask you to consider their role in securing Stalin's control over every aspect of Soviet society or the extent to which the later purges were a continuation of, or departure from, Lenin's policies.

Essential notes

Yagoda's fall from power is an example of Stalin's tactic of blaming others for supposed excesses. Stalin's appointment of Yezhov as head of the NKVD in 1936 began an escalation of the purges and the beginning of the Great Terror of 1936–9.

The Great Terror, 1936–9

By 1936, Stalin had achieved extensive control over both the party and the country. Nevertheless, he ordered an escalation of the purges, claiming in speeches that there were enemies both inside and outside the USSR. The purges during the years 1936–9, which historian Robert Conquest has called the 'Great Terror', saw a far wider persecution, and the execution of prominent political leaders.

Fall of Yagoda

Following the trial of Zinoviev and Kamenev, Yagoda was removed from his post of head of the NKVD and replaced by Nikolai Yezhov. Stalin had never trusted Yagoda. An earlier report had suggested that Yagoda supported Bukharin and the right of the party. Stalin believed that he had been insufficiently aggressive in the aftermath of the death of Kirov, and again in his handling of the first Moscow Show Trial of Zinoviev and Kamenev.

Purge of the NKVD

Stalin believed that the NKVD had not been ruthless enough in exposing enemies of the state, suggesting the organisation was 'four years behind'. In 1937, he ordered a purge of the NKVD itself, eliminating older members whose loyalty to him personally was questionable, much as he had done in the party with the purge of Old Bolsheviks. An estimated 3000 NKVD staff died.

A quota system was introduced, resembling those of the Five-Year Plans. The new recruits were ambitious to advance their careers. In order to meet targets they arrested many innocent people. There was no appeal against arrest, and execution was often carried out straight away. The new head, Yezhov, directed the NKVD during this period when the Secret Police arrested ever more supposed enemies of the state just when it was likely that real enemies were at their fewest.

Purge of the party

Purge of the right: Trial of the 17

In the Trial of the 17 in 1937, the accused included Karl Radek and Grigory Sokolnikov, labelled the 'anti-Soviet Trotskyite Centre'. This Second Moscow Show Trial was the first time Yezhov's new system of what is sometimes called 'conveyor belt interrogation' was used. This involved a ceaseless cycle of torture, sleep deprivation and questioning at the hands of different officials until the victim confessed. Radek avoided execution by confessing, implicating Bukharin. Thirteen of his fellow defendants were executed; the remaining four, including Radek himself, were sent to prison camps, where they died.

Third Moscow Show Trial: Trial of the 21

The confessions of Zinoviev and Kamenev in the First Moscow Show Trial had implicated the right of the party. Bukharin, Rykov and Tomsky were accordingly investigated; Tomsky committed suicide before formal charges could be made. The case against Bukharin and Rykov had been strengthened during the Second Moscow Show Trial.

In 1938, Yezhov moved against Bukharin and Rykov. They and 19 others (including the disgraced Yagoda) were publicly prosecuted in the third of the Moscow Show Trials. The defendants were charged with attempting to overthrow the government of the Soviet Union. Bukharin was charged with the attempted assassination of Lenin. Bukharin refused to acknowledge his guilt for the crimes of which he was accused, although he did agree to 'political responsibility'. Bukharin, Rykov, Yagoda and the remaining 18 were executed shortly after the trial. The Show Trials eliminated Stalin's old adversaries and critics, but also allies such as Yagoda from whom it was now politically convenient to distance himself. Concurrent purges targeted the younger members of the party. From 1934 until 1938, 330 000 party members were condemned as class enemies.

Purge of the army

Stalin knew he was not in total command of the USSR as long as the armed forces retained so much autonomy. He also knew that the top military personnel had been appointed by Trotsky as Commissar for War.

In 1937 Chief of General Staff Marshal Mikhail Tukhachevsky and seven generals were charged with spying for Germany and Japan. They were tortured, tried in secret and executed. Almost all the Army Commanders and two thirds of commanders lost their positions; 35 000 officers were incarcerated or executed. The purge of the army was complete by 1939.

In the Soviet navy all serving admirals were shot, and thousands of naval officers were deported to the labour camps.

All but one of the senior air force commanders died.

Purge of the people

During the Show Trials, the Soviet authorities concluded that there was widespread sedition among ordinary people in the USSR. The purge was extended: NKVD Order No. 00447 required the elimination of 'anti-Soviet elements' from society. To this end, the Secret Police produced a list of 250 000 people who could be considered class enemies. Motivated by ambition or fear, ordinary Russians denounced neighbours, friends and work colleagues. The Great Terror enabled Stalin to achieve absolute control over all aspects of Soviet society.

Examiners' notes

You will find that different history books use three phrases to refer to this period: 'Great Purge', 'Great Terror' and 'Yezhovshchina'. The first two of these names indicates that this was the most murderous of the purges. The third names the period after Yezhov, the head of the NKVD who directed the purges at this time. When answering an exam question, you can use all three expressions.

Essential notes

One key consequence of the purges was the undermining of the army and near-destruction of the officer corps (historians disagree over how extensive this was). Such a result was good for a dictator afraid of a coup, but disastrous in what turned out to be the run-up to a major war. (See also pages 58–61 for more on this point.)

Impact of the Great Terror

The most notable characteristic of the Terror was how comprehensive it was. Few people in the Soviet Union, whatever their social status, were unaffected. It is difficult to estimate the number of deaths that occurred as a consequence of the purges, and historians do not agree:

- Robert Conquest and Simon Sebag Montefiore estimate 20 million.
- Alec Nove and Stephen Wheatcroft suggest 4 million – 11 million.
- Declassified Soviet archives record that in 1937–8 there were 1000 executions a day, which is probably an underestimate.

Social impact

After Kirov's murder, the initial focus was on the Leningrad Party but was soon extended to every section of the party, every part of the country and every group of the population. Eventually, every national republic was affected: in Stalin's native Georgia, historians argue that 80 000 were executed. Every social class was touched, but skilled workers and the intelligentsia – managers, scientists, engineers, historians, artists and writers – appear to be have been targeted more than manual workers, telling us from where Stalin and the NKVD thought the threat would come.

As well as this, the families of those arrested were targeted: Radek's and Ryutin's family were executed. Even when left alive, the children of enemies of the state were often excluded from university and the professions.

In addition, Alexander Yakovlev and Michael Ellman have shown that the attack on the church escalated. Yakovlev suggests that 100 000 priests, monks and nuns may have died in 1937–8.

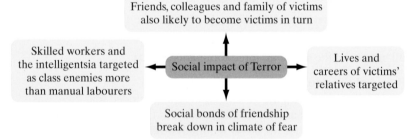

How the Terror affected every aspect of life

Economic impact

In the workplace Communist Party officials and factory managers lied about production levels in order to avoid arrest when targets were not met.

Purges within *Gosplan* removed some of the most distinguished economists and economic planners. Accurate economic planning was impossible as a result, and the poor economic performance hindered the preparation for war at a time when German rearmament was well advanced. The Terror removed managers, technicians and statisticians, leading to a shortage of professional expertise. Skilled workers were also targeted, accused of being 'wreckers' or saboteurs.

The height of the purges coincided with (and undoubtedly contributed to) the economic slowdown that began in 1937. Alec Nove blames the downturn directly on the purges, which jettisoned experienced personnel.

How the Terror affected the economy

Political impact

By the end of the Great Terror in 1939, Stalin had achieved unrivalled political dominance. He had established a personal dictatorship. Under Stalin, terror became a routine and total method of control. He had destroyed all leading political opponents within the Soviet Union (Trotsky was in exile, to be assassinated in 1940), including:

- older communists with a long history in the party

- remaining members of Lenin's first government

- those who had competed for leadership of the Soviet Union in 1920s

- any who had supported Trotsky in the 1920s but then confessed and conformed

- those who had opposed Stalin earlier in the 1930s.

The party was now an organisation that could approve Stalin's decisions, but could not discuss, restrain or oppose them.

Towards a totalitarian state

By the end of the 1930s Stalin had established a totalitarian state. He had a stranglehold on the party. Through his purge of the military, Stalin had cowed an institution with the potential to challenge his rule. He kept the Secret Police under control, changing leaders and ensuring rank and file NKVD men were loyal to him. The Terror had also insulated him from the consequences of his actions as there were always scapegoats to blame for the shortcomings of his policies.

While one of the main consequences of the Terror was the establishment of Stalin's political and social dominance, there were other outcomes (see the diagram on the right).

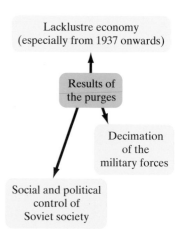

Results of the purges

The later purges, 1941–53

The Terror had reached its height 1937–8; at the 18th Party Congress in 1939, Stalin declared an end to the Great Purge. Despite this, in the 15 years up to his death in 1953, purges formed a central part of Stalin's system as a means of both political and social control.

Role of Beria

Lavrentiy Beria followed Yezhov as head of the NKVD after the latter's arrest in 1938 and was head of the Secret Police until 1953. He was one of Stalin's closest associates and oversaw all of the later purges. His first major campaign was against Yezhov: in 1940, his predecessor was executed, along with 346 of his associates.

Armed forces

Despite Stalin's declaring an end to the Great Purge, the purge of the military continued even after the 1941 German invasion. The attention of the NKVD turned to military-intelligence officers, whom Stalin blamed for not warning him of the Nazi attack (though they had; he had believed his own diplomacy, including the non-aggression pact of 1939, would indefinitely postpone any attack).

Defeats and setbacks in the 'Great Patriotic War' were blamed on traitors, saboteurs and incompetence. Several generals were shot for retreating; others committed suicide rather than face execution. This approach depleted the Red Army of vital military expertise. Eventually the purge of the armed forces was abandoned as it was hindering the Soviet war effort.

Enemy within

Large numbers of the non-Russian ethnic minorities, who might see the German troops as liberators from Russian or Soviet rule, were shot. Beria ordered the NKVD execution squads to double their efforts to deal with this problem. Executions had usually happened at night; Beria ordered that his officers kill victims both day and night to ensure enough people were being murdered. He was also given the job of moving entire populations of ethnic minorities from the European west, where the Germans were advancing, to the Asian east of the country where they could not collaborate with the invaders. Kalmyks, Chechens, Crimean Tartars, ethnic Germans and others were moved to Altai Krai, Kazakhstan and remote parts of Siberia.

Purge of the Jews

Suspicious of Western influence during the war, after 1945 Stalin launched a campaign against 'cosmopolitanism'. In practical terms this entailed a purge of the Jewish population. Between 1945 and 1951, Jews who held important and influential positions in government, industry, the military, the diplomatic corps, the arts and the professions were purged. In 1945, 12 per cent of senior managers in industry and government were Jewish; this figure had shrunk to 4 per cent by 1951.

Leningrad Affair

The Leningrad Affair of 1949 was almost Stalin's final purge. It followed the death in 1948 of Zhdanov, a favourite of Stalin's and Leningrad Party boss.

Stalin had long been suspicious of the Leningrad Party: the city was closely associated in Stalin's mind with Zinoviev and Kirov. Beria was ordered to investigate party members. As a consequence, 1000 Communist Party members were expelled and, of these, 200 were arrested and shot. Those executed included Kuznetsov, hero of the 1941–4 Siege of Leningrad, and others who had been awarded the title 'Hero of the Soviet Union'.

Doctors' Plot

In his final months, Stalin became convinced that his closest associates were trying to kill him. In January 1953, nine doctors were accused of having killed Zhdanov and other high-ranking communists, and of planning to murder Stalin. Two of the nine died in custody; all had signed confessions admitting to the charges.

Seven of the nine arrested were Jewish: this was almost certainly an anti-Semitic purge ordered by Stalin, who had been expressing hostility to Jews for years. His anti-Semitism may have been given further impetus by the 1948 foundation of the State of Israel, which the USA had been the first to recognise. Some historians have suggested that a mass deportation or mass execution of Soviet Jews was in preparation at the time of Stalin's death.

Stalin died before executions of the remaining doctors could take place. The supposed plot was then declared 'a fabrication' and MVD (formerly the NKVD) officials were executed for their role in this episode.

Unfettered dictatorship

By this late stage of his rule, there was little attempt to disguise the fact that there were no restraints on Stalin. His was a totalitarian regime. From 1947, the much-purged Central Committee of the Soviet Union barely played a role; it was only to rediscover a political life following Stalin's death. Nevertheless, he remained constantly on the watch for heirs and rivals: the popularity of the heroes of the Siege of Leningrad may have been enough to doom them. It is possible that Stalin was preparing to move against Beria, as he had earlier against Yagoda and Yezhov.

Examiners' notes

In answering exam questions relating to the purges, it is worth making a distinction between the different stages. For example, earlier purges had removed enemies of the Bolshevik regime, then dissidents within the Communist Party, then Stalin's enemies and supposed enemies. Fewer people died in the later purges than in the Great Terror. You should explain that the purges demonstrate the extent to which terror had begun to affect the entire system.

Involvement of party members in USSR and abroad: tied party functionaries' careers and lives to Stalin

Scapegoating of figures involved in earlier purges: Yagoda himself tried and executed

A belief in conspiracies and menace: good for national unity

What did the purge achieve?

An atmosphere of intimidation: good for discipline of the party

Increased Stalin's power and control: good for Stalin's leadership

Public confessions by the accused appeared to confirm reality of the menace: leading figures at home and abroad approve the process as legal and just

Stalin's control spread by means of purges and collectivisation

Stalin and culture

Social realism

The Bolshevik Revolution had coincided with a period of experimentation in the arts. Radical in their own work, many artists supported the dramatic changes of 1917. Some genuinely tried to create revolutionary work. Some Bolsheviks supported artistic freedom; Stalin declared that artists were 'engineers of the human soul'. Under his rule, the arts were required to illustrate a vision of a socialist society and help in the creation of a new Soviet man.

Radical artists in the years just before and just after the 1917 Revolution had been as revolutionary in their way as the Bolsheviks; like them, artists confidently tried new methods that startled and shocked some people. Under Stalin, the state insisted that they return to a largely photographic style of representational art called social realism. This doctrine demanded that artists depict neither what they saw taking place nor what they really thought about what they actually saw, but a vision of a future socialist state.

- Art was to be positive about the present and optimistic about the future.
- All representations of the USSR, its officials and people were to be benign and attractive.
- Ugliness and distortion were restricted to satirical cartoons attacking the capitalist West.

In Zhdanov's words, art 'should be able to portray our heroes; it should be able to glimpse our tomorrow'.

Art

In 1929, the All-Union Cooperative of Workers in Representational Art was formed. The establishment of the Committee for Art Affairs (KPDI) under the direction of Yezhov enforced adherence to social realist principles. The 1930s saw countless paintings of three topics:

- peasants on collective farms
- industrial workers
- Stalin.

A Kolkhoz Celebration by Sergey Gerasimov show a rural life that is prosperous, clean, orderly and amicable; the realities of collectivisation are ignored.

A Kolkhoz Celebration by Sergey Gerasimov 1937

In the era of Stakhanovism, paintings often focused on the heroic efforts of industrial workers in the Five-Year Plans. *To Storm the Third Year of the Five-Year Plan* by Gustav Klutsis is clearly a propaganda poster designed to inspire workers to greater efforts.

Gustav Klutsis' 1930 poster *To Storm the Third Year of the Five-Year Plan*

Vera Mukhina's sculpture *Industrial Worker and Collective Farm Girl* represented the alliance between the proletariat and peasantry. Designed for the Soviet Pavilion at the 1937 Paris Expo, the two figures stride in step symbolising unity of purpose. They raise the implements of their work, which are also the emblems of the Soviet state. A colossal sculpture made with 60 tonnes of stainless steel, it was set up outside the All-Russia Exhibition Centre and received Stalin's personal approval.

Industrial Worker and Collective Farm Girl by Vera Mukhina, 1937

☞ Continued on the next two pages

Examiners' notes

Social realism could also be used to demonstrate that Stalin's regime was totalitarian, as it was a form of control and propaganda.

Essential notes

A *smychka* or 'alliance' between peasantry and proletariat had overthrown the old regime. In his last works, Lenin had written of the importance of winning the (majority) peasants' trust. Bukharin, Rykov and the right argued for concessions to win them over. The left feared that hostility to change and the desire to own land would kill off the revolution and accordingly opposed compromise. Mukhina's icon suggests the problem no longer exists.

Grigori Shegal's portrait of Stalin entitled *Leader, Teacher, Friend* subtly establishes in the viewer's mind that Stalin was Lenin's disciple by placing the dead revolutionary's statue just behind the Secretary-General, seeming to look on approvingly. These paintings preach that Stalin was Lenin's closest ally in life, and only heir in death; they thus reinforce the work of the Show Trials.

Leader, Teacher, Friend by G. M. Shegal, 1937

Architecture

In 1931 the Union of Architects was formed. All members were expected to conform to the standards of socialist architecture, designing buildings able to rouse Soviet spirits. The famous Moscow Metro, finished in 1935 as part of the Second Five-Year Plan, was designed as a series of palaces. In 1934, a proposal to build a 300-metre tower crowned by a 100-metre statue of Lenin won an architectural competition to design the 'Palace of the Soviets'. (The project was never completed.)

Literature

In 1932, the Russian Association of Proletarian Writers was replaced by the Union of Soviet Writers nominally headed by Maxim Gorky. Novelists had to adhere to strict rules. Fyodor Gladkov's *Cement* tells of how a group of demobilised Red Army soldiers build a cement works. Nicolai Ostrovsky's tellingly entitled *How the Steel Was Tempered* was said to be the most borrowed book from the library in Magnitogorsk in 1934. Writers such as Boris Pasternak and the poet Anna Akhmatova, who refused to conform to the new orthodoxy, were in constant danger.

Music

The Union of Soviet Composers was founded in 1932 to regulate composers and music. Avant-garde and experimental music were banned. Shostakovich's 1934 opera *Lady Macbeth of the Mtensk District* was badly reviewed in *Pravda*, possibly by Stalin himself. The dictator may have taken offence at the story of adultery and murder, and the sympathy for the central character, who commits both crimes. But the review, entitled 'Chaos instead of music' complained of the 'farrago of chaotic, nonsensical sounds'. Before the first performance of his carefully conservative fifth symphony, the composer published an article in which he referred to it as 'a Soviet artist's creative response to justified criticism'.

Jazz was performed from the 1920s, but suffered in the 1940s as an example of 'cosmopolitanism' in music.

Cinema and theatre

In the 1930s the Politburo controlled filmmaking and new films were previewed by the State Committee for Cinematography. Films had to be presented in a form accessible to the masses. Documentaries told mass audiences of the industrial successes of the Five-Year Plans. *Three Songs about Lenin*, a 1934 film by Dziga Vertov in which three songs are sung by unknown Soviet citizens praising Lenin, was held up as an exemplar of social realist cinematography. Stalin sometimes chose the subject of a film. He especially loved films that portrayed him as a hero in the civil war.

All experimental work trying new, shocking, startling or unexpected approaches was rejected. So was realism (as opposed to official 'social' realism). Thus, Meyerhold's Theatre, Jewish Theatre of Solomon Mikhoels and Tairov's Chamber Theatre were suppressed, the actors and directors exiled to Siberia.

The role of social realism

Essential notes

Pasternak died in a labour camp after writing a poem criticising Stalin (which Yagoda admired and recited to Stalin from memory, perhaps unwisely). In the years after 1922 Akhmatova was condemned as a bourgeois element and was later persecuted by the regime and prevented from publishing anything new.

Examiners' notes

Good answers show that students can apply their knowledge wherever it serves their argument, and you may be able to use cultural material to back up points about wartime victory, the personality cult, the economic and social changes, etc.

Essential notes

See page 52 regarding the emphasis on prosperity, social cohesion and progress in social realism.

Cult of personality

The cult of personality contributed to the creation of a totalitarian state and helped secure Stalin's personal dictatorship. Following the German invasion in 1941, known as Operation Barbarossa, it played an important part in the war effort. The constant emphasis in portraits, fiction and films on Stalin's connection with Lenin, his wisdom and personal modesty, placed him above politics. Some historians have argued that propaganda was as important as purges to defending the regime.

Portraits of Stalin were one of three frequently recurring topics in the regulated world of social realist art. In this way the use of the arts as propaganda helped to develop Stalin's cult of personality. It was impossible to present a vision of a socialist society without Stalin as its central character. This formed part of the optimism and loyalty that were all part of the regime's propaganda in establishing and maintaining a totalitarian state.

Like social realism itself, the cult:

- demonstrated and thus supported the political, economic and social goals of the regime

- affirmed and thus consolidated Stalin's personal rule.

The cult of personality developed in stages, reaching its peak in the years following the Second World War.

Stage 1: Lenin's disciple (1924–9)

The cult began immediately following Lenin's death in January 1924. The cult of Lenin, which had begun during his lifetime, reached new heights after his death, with the Soviet authorities embalming his body for public display. Stalin capitalised upon this first by delivering the eulogy at Lenin's funeral and then by presenting himself as Lenin's loyal co-worker.

Photographs (sometimes doctored) appeared showing Lenin in Stalin's company, demonstrating the close collaboration between them. Old Bolsheviks were erased from group photographs ahead of publication, so that visual evidence of Lenin's closeness to rivals who lost the leadership struggle, notably Trotsky, was eliminated. Thus propaganda created a clear link between Stalin and Lenin in the public mind even while apparently promoting the official cult of Lenin.

Stage 2: Lenin's equal (1929–33)

Stalin's 50th birthday celebrations in December 1929 were stage-managed to merge with commemorations of Lenin's death in January 1930. While he was still portrayed as Lenin's follower, his stature was allowed to grow to equal Lenin's. A private birthday celebration with prominent party members took place in the shadow of a statue of Lenin.

Images of Stalin and Lenin were set side by side in posters and newspapers for public consumption. The clear message was that the two men were equal in their importance to the communist movement. This was in contrast to the earlier images of the 1920s where, in propaganda posters, a smaller Stalin was placed reverentially behind a dominating image of Lenin. Applause at party conferences following Stalin's speech grew longer, with no party member wanting to be seen to stop first.

Stage 3: Stalin's wisdom (1933–9)

The cult of personality was fully established during these years. Stalin carefully cultivated an image as an avuncular figure whom the people could trust:

- he was one of them

- he was not wealthy (not corrupt, took no bribes)

- he lived modestly.

By cultivating this persona as a man of the people, Stalin claimed his authority to rule on their behalf. People viewed Stalin as a symbol of stability in the turbulent years of collectivisation and the Five-Year Plans.

Stage 4: Stalin's cult of personality (1945–53)

Stalin emerged from the war with his reputation enhanced. Credited with transforming a backward agricultural nation into an industrial and military giant, he was also the victorious wartime leader. As before, Stalin took care to safeguard his image: paintings glorifying Stalin's role in the USSR's victory decorated public buildings. In the official histories, the Soviet people could not have defeated the Germans without him. The 1947 edition of his biography offered breathless praise:

> 'His work is extraordinary for its variety; his energy truly amazing. The range of questions which engage his attention is immense. Stalin is wise and deliberate in solving complex political questions … he is a supreme master of bold revolutionary decisions … Stalin is the Lenin of today.'

The section of the biography on the Great Patriotic War does not acknowledge the contribution of military commanders, such as Marshal Zhukov. Propaganda identified the country with the party, and the party with Stalin. The country was now one of the world's two superpowers and Stalin one of the world's most powerful men. By the time of his 70th birthday in 1949, Stalin's power was at its height: he was seen as the man who had saved Russia from Germany and communism from Nazism, created an empire in Eastern Europe and achieved nuclear parity with America.

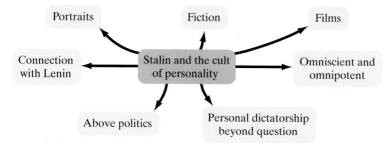

Stalin and the cult of personality

Essential notes

In *Pravda*, the leading Soviet newspaper, Stalin was frequently referred to as the 'Master of Wisdom' or the 'Wisest Man of Our Times'. Paintings, poetry, fiction and film all portrayed Stalin as a hero of the revolutionary years. The *History of the Communist Party of the Soviet Union: Short Course* (1938) rewrote history to give Stalin a pivotal role in the Bolshevik Revolution.

Essential notes

Historian Roy Medvedev argues: 'Stalin did not rely on terror alone, but also on the support of the majority of the people; effectively deceived by cunning propaganda, they gave Stalin credit for the services of others and even for "achievements" that were in fact totally fictitious'.

Preparation for war

Foreign policy	Domestic policy	Internal security policy

• End isolation
  – Seek allies
• Postpone conflict
  – Sign non-aggression pact
• Build up network of spies
	• Build up domestic strength
	  – Import Western technology
	  – Develop heavy industry in 5YPs
	  – Prioritise armaments in 5YPs
		• Crush all opposition
		• Suppress all internal division
		• Infiltrate NKVD into all parts of society and economy

Stalin's preparation for war

Essential notes

That the USA, France and Great Britain had supported the Whites in the civil war only contributed to mutual suspicion.

Foreign policy situation, 1924

Following the revolution, Russia had been vulnerable as the world's only communist country. Lenin's foreign policy had been pragmatic, acknowledging that:

• Russia was isolated, with enemies and no friends among nations

• Russia needed Western technology for industrialisation.

This pragmatism brought results. Russia withdrew from the First World War, and went on to sign a trade agreement with Britain and a military agreement with Germany.

Threat from Germany

There was every reason for Stalin to fear Germany:

• Germany had beaten Russia in the First World War.

• From 1933 the country was led by Adolf Hitler, a vocal anti-communist.

• Under Hitler, Germany had begun rapidly building up its armed forces.

• Soon after becoming the German Chancellor, Hitler had taken several aggressive and expansionist steps.

Stalin initially retained Lenin's Foreign Commissar Georgy Chicherin and his policy of peaceful coexistence. However, in 1934 Hitler cancelled the 1926 agreement for military cooperation with the USSR and signed a non-aggression pact with Poland. Stalin directed the new Foreign Commissar Maxim Litvinov to end Soviet isolation by joining the League of Nations and signing a Mutual Assistance Pact with France and Czechoslovakia in 1935, each guaranteeing to aid the others in the event of an attack on any one of them.

In 1936, the threat from Germany was amplified with the formation of the Anti-Comintern Pact. This was an alliance between Nazi Germany and Imperial Japan, formed in November 1936, joined in 1937 by Fascist Italy; they were later to be the three Axis Powers.

In the Spanish Civil War (1936–9), the USSR and Germany backed different sides, adding to the sense that war between the Nazi and communist states was inevitable.

When Hitler threatened Czechoslovakia in 1938, the British, seeking to avoid or postpone war, signed the Munich Agreement, allowing Germany to occupy part of Czechoslovakia. Stalin interpreted this as giving Hitler permission to pursue his declared expansionist ambitions.

Litvinov also tried to build an alliance against Germany. This attempt to pursue a 'collective security' failed because however much they distrusted Hitler and feared Germany, the major Western powers also:

- distrusted Stalin
- feared communism
- regarded Nazi Germany as a fellow opponent of communism.

Stalin interpreted the 1938 Munich Agreement as Britain giving Hitler permission to pursue his declared expansionist ambitions in Eastern Europe.

The French and the British ignored Litvinov's overtures following the Munich Agreement. Isolated and badly prepared for war, Stalin gave his new Foreign Commissar Molotov permission to enter into an agreement with Germany. Historian Robert Service sees the agreement as a way of buying time, and that Stalin believed the pact would delay war with Germany until 1943. In August 1939, the Nazi–Soviet Non-Aggression Pact was signed. This pact is also known by the names of the two Foreign Ministers who were its signatories – the Ribbentrop–Molotov Pact. This stated:

- Germany and the USSR would be neutral if either is in conflict with other countries
- USSR would be free to recapture lands ceded in 1918: Bessarabia, Estonia, Finland, Latvia, Lithuania and eastern Poland
- USSR would provide Germany with raw materials and grain.

Domestic preparations: reform of the military

Reform of the military

At the outbreak of war, the USSR was not well prepared to defend itself. After Trotsky's 1925 dismissal as Commissar for War, the size of the army had fallen below 600 000 soldiers. Stalin appointed as War Commissar Kliment Voroshilov, who had been active in the Great Terror, denouncing colleagues.

Although discipline was emphasised, new conscripts to the military were inevitably poorly educated peasants and workers. Stalin reintroduced the army ranks that had been used under the Tsars but abolished by the Bolsheviks.

As intended, the 1937–8 purge of the Red Army eliminated the only people capable of overthrowing Stalin. However, it also removed the army's leading military strategists and experts, including Marshal Mikhail Tukhachevsky. Voroshilov led the army into the Winter War (1939–40) against Finland, in which it tellingly suffered massive casualties. At the time of Operation Barbarossa, Beria was leading the NKVD in a new purge of the army (1940–2) in which still further senior officers were arrested. Even after 1941 it took time for Stalin both to call a halt to purging the armed forces and to allow his top military personnel sufficient autonomy in decision-making.

Course of the war

Operation Barbarossa

The German invasion of the Soviet Union began on 22 June 1941. Hitler had always intended to launch an attack on the Soviet Union and Stalin had been aware of plans for an attack as early as 1935. But the timing of the German attack took Stalin by surprise.

Problems of 1941: Stalin's leadership

Stalin received numerous warnings that an attack must be imminent from three key sources:

- Military intelligence had kept Stalin briefed that Germany was mobilising troops along Soviet borders.
- Communist sympathisers in different countries gave the USSR a network of spies.
- Foreign governments sent reports: British intelligence informed Stalin of Hitler's plans.

Stalin rejected all such reports as disinformation, refusing to believe that Hitler would risk fighting a war on two fronts. Soviet forces were not allowed to respond in any way that the Germans would interpret as confrontational. When the attack did happen, Stalin stayed in his country house, out of contact. These early days exposed Stalin's greatest error: misjudgement of Hitler's actions and intentions. This, together with his ill-judged and ill-timed purge of the armed forces, amounted to a colossal failure of leadership.

Problems of 1941: the condition of the army

Germany fielded an experienced and well-trained force was mobile and well prepared, with good communications, and a ruthless approach to the conquered population.

The Soviet forces were not ready to withstand such a well-planned surprise attack. Recent fighting with Poland and Finland, and the earlier civil war, meant that the army was by no means inexperienced. However the purges had removed too many commanders and the troops lacked competent leaders: too many of those in charge owed their promotion more to their political than their military qualities.

Even the diplomatic successes of the Ribbentrop–Molotov Pact caused problems: much of the army was now in the middle of Poland, in territory that did not provide natural defences.

In addition, Stalin's command to provide Germany with no pretext for attack left commanders in the field unable to respond to the emergency. Worse, for the first two days after the attack Stalin remained out of contact, issuing no instructions. In the centralised system he had designed, amid the climate of fear he had created, no one was willing to take any initiative. The situation was made worse when orders finally arrived not to retreat: units that could have redeployed to more defensible ground were cut off and annihilated.

Finally, the continuing focus of the economy on quotas meant that while armaments were available, the emphasis on quantity rather than quality meant that they were prone to breaking down, leaving them vulnerable to German air force and artillery. Huge numbers of tanks were lost and more than 2.4 million men had been captured by December 1941, with the invaders approaching the outskirts of the capital.

Stalin's recovery of nerve

Stalin recovered and on 3 July 1941 broadcast a rousing speech calling on the people of the Soviet Union to defend their country. Understanding that they would see the German advance as an attack on their home, not on their political system, he shrewdly appealed not to their communist sympathies but to their Russian patriotism. He accepted Marshal Zhukov's assurance that Moscow would not fall to the Germans and remained in the capital. Foreign Commissar Molotov suggested that defeat would have been certain had Stalin fled Moscow, such would have been the blow to morale.

Examiners' notes

In addressing questions on the importance of Stalin's leadership to the outcome of the war you may need to put the issue into context by noting the important contribution of key military leaders, prominent among them Zhukov.

Soviet successes

Date	German name for operation	Name of battle	Significance
January 1941 to January 1944	Operation Barbarossa	Siege of Leningrad	Zhukov's leadership was key. The siege lasted 28 months and caused massive loss of life. Over 700 000 inhabitants died of hypothermia or starvation. The attack failed. The former capital, one of the country's two most important cities, remained in Soviet hands.
September 1941	Operation Typhoon	Battle of Moscow	After initial panic, Muscovites settled to digging anti-tank trenches in the freezing earth by hand. Zhukov embarked on a successful counter-attack and pushed German forces back 200 km. The Germans had lost their best opportunity to capture the capital city.
June 1942 to January 1943	Operation Blue	Battle of Stalingrad	Stalin ordered the city to which he gave his name be defended at all costs. The battle lasted six months, over 1 million Soviet soldiers died in house-to-house fighting. By the winter, massive Russian reinforcements were in place commanded by Zhukov. Hitler was forced to deploy troops from other theatres of operations. German forces surrendered after vast losses. The Soviet victory was a turning point in the war.
July 1943	Operation Citadel	Battle of Kursk	The biggest tank battle ever witnessed. 700 000 German troops faced 1.3 million Soviet forces who were aided by superior tank and aircraft numbers. Hitler accepted the need for retreat and Operation Citadel was aborted. Another crushing Soviet victory.

By the end of the war, the Soviets had retaken all the parts of the USSR that the Germans had occupied. But more than that, the Red Army had overrun Bulgaria, Czechoslovakia, part of Germany, Hungary, Poland and Romania. Stalin had begun to establish a central and east European empire. In addition, following the Yalta Agreement, the Soviet Union declared war on Japan, attacking the Japanese troops in Manchuria.

Social impact of the war

The social impact of the Second World War on the USSR

Human cost of war

It is estimated that in the USSR 4 million people died in the first year of the conflict alone. By the end of the war, estimates suggest anywhere from 10 to 30 million people had died. A third of these were military personnel; the rest were civilians. Soviet losses are generally estimated as more than double the total number of casualties from Britain, France, America and Germany combined. In addition, by the end of 1941, as much as half the population of the USSR lived under German rule.

Starvation accounted for at least a quarter of these deaths. Food shortages continued throughout the war. People boiled nettles for tea, hunted dogs, cats and rats for food and even resorted to cannibalism (during the Siege of Leningrad, 226 people were arrested for cannibalism).

As the war progressed, its impact on ordinary Soviet citizens worsened. The Soviet authorities neglected the agricultural economy. The lack of both machinery and labour meant a drastic decrease in the supply of food. Food was rationed, and there were official quantities of specific food that workers were supposed to be given. However, the actual amount supplied rarely reached official levels while rural consumption of even the most basic foodstuffs like bread and potatoes declined.

Work in the war

Because of the war, the Soviet people worked in even worse conditions than usual. Industry was directed towards the war effort, shortages were acute and queues were long: the motto was 'Everything for the Front'. By 1942, the Soviet Union spent more than half its national income on defence, far more than any other participant in the Second World War. All fit adults who did not work in essential industries were conscripted into the military.

Agriculture suffered as tractor stations and factories were converted to tank and aircraft production. Production of food now required backbreaking work, done for the most part by those assessed as unfit for military service – often the old. Fields were ploughed and harvested by hand. Under such conditions, collective farms were unable to feed the Soviet population.

In the factories, industrial workers were expected to work seven days a week with shifts of 12–18 hours per day. Workers undertaking hard manual labour had a diet that failed to give them the calories they needed. Discipline was harsh: the NKVD punishments for not working hard enough or arriving late were severe.

Women in the war

With so many able-bodied men in the military, women came to form the majority of the workforce in the Soviet Union during the war: by 1945, they were 56 per cent of the workforce. In areas where men had been conscripted to fight and factories evacuated, they made up even higher percentages. Few were promoted to management.

In agriculture, there were neither enough tractors nor enough draught animals, so women were often harnessed to pull farm machinery. The proportion of women in the agricultural labour force doubled from 40 per cent before the war to 80 per cent by the end.

They contributed to the country's defence, building anti-tank trenches and serving in the fire services in towns and cities. There were a million women serving in the Soviet armed forces, although few achieved high rank. There were distinguished female pilots such as Marina Raskova, as well as all-female companies of fighters and bombers. Women also trained and served as snipers.

Despite this, propaganda during and after the war mainly praised women's contribution to the workforce and family; pictures of women in uniform and fighting were kept from publication.

USSR in 1945

The Soviet Union emerged from the war victorious:

- National unity was maintained: the Red Army held together as a fighting force and the USSR survived as a state.

- The nation had stuck to its determination to win at all costs. There had been terrible loss of civilian and military life, and vast economic damage.

- The populace had contributed hugely to the war effort. Without their continued sacrifice and effort, no amount of military genius by Zhukov or political shrewdness by Stalin could have achieved the final victory in the Great Patriotic War. Their suffering had been even greater than in the 1930s with Stalin's lethal policies of collectivisation and industrialisation.

Even though it emerged victorious in 1945, the situation in the Soviet Union at the end of the war was grim. Although the USSR was now an acknowledged economic and military giant, the partner of Great Britain and the USA at the major conferences of the war, the standard of living for the majority of the population was the lowest it had been since 1917.

Examiners' notes

You will need to note both economic failures and successes under Stalin. Questions may require you to understand the transformation of the USSR from the devastation of the years 1941–2 to the global economic superpower that emerged from the war.

Economic impact of the war

Economic disaster 1941–2

Economically, the Great Patriotic War had a dramatic impact on the Soviet Union in the year following the German invasion. Some analysts claim that the gains made under the Five-Year Plans were lost in the first years of the war.

- By 1942, industrial production had dropped to 40 per cent below 1940 levels. Not surprisingly, since about a third of the industry had fallen into German hands.

- Production of coal, iron, steel and electricity–all vital to munitions and weaponry – roughly halved in this period.

- Much of the population lost its electricity supply for the duration of the war.

- A little under half of the railway system was out of action.

- In 1942 production of grain was down to less than half of what it had been in 1940 as about a third of the country's agriculture, including the most fertile agricultural areas (notably Ukraine), were overrun by the invading German army. The country had also lost nearly half of its cattle and over half its pigs.

- Both agriculture and industry were naturally affected by the massive conscription programme that took millions of men out of the workplace and into fighting.

The retreating Red Army had carried out a scorched-earth policy to ensure the conquering Germans found as little supplies as possible in 1941. The German forces adopted the same tactic when they pulled back in 1943–4. As a result, countless buildings and bridges had been destroyed in both towns and countryside.

Economic recovery 1942–5

After the disasters of 1941, the economy recovered dramatically. By 1944 the total industrial output exceeded that of 1940. Many historians are willing to give credit to Stalin's decisions at this stage. Following the German invasion, Stalin ordered that the surviving industrial plant be relocated east of the Ural Mountains. A Council for Evacuation was established in July 1941 to oversee the planning and implementation. The command economy Stalin had established to implement the Five-Year Plans now proved that in wartime it could act effectively.

Between July and December 1941, more than 2500 industrial units were moved to a safer distance from the front, for example, ten Leningrad munitions factories were moved to Magnitogorsk. With the German army on its outskirts, the people of Zaporozhe, Ukraine, dismantled the industrial plant of the city, loaded it all on to nearly 10 000 goods wagons (along with instructions for reconstruction) and sent the trains away before the town fell to the invaders.

Hundreds of thousands of workers were evacuated along with the factories where they worked. For example, 350 000 workers were evacuated from Kiev. Some factories were reassembled and in production very quickly. A relocated Kharkov tractor factory began producing tanks for the Soviet frontlines as early as December 1941. Most evacuated factories were in production by 1943.

Economic power

The wartime relocation of the economy allowed the Soviet Union's industrial production to first recover pre-war levels, and then to exceed them. The USSR emerged from the war as an industrial and military superpower. The economic achievements of the USSR in the last three years of the war represented the pinnacle of efficiency and success. In 1943, for example, military production surpassed German efforts.

There were a number of reasons why the Soviet Union was able to enact such a radical transformation:

- Centralised decision-making allowed binding decisions to be made quickly and with minimum debate.
- Command economy structures allowed for the swift implementation of policy.
- Industrial expenditure was already heavily weighted to heavy industry and defence.
- Purges and the terrifying discipline of the Five-Year Plans and collectivisation had created a compliant workforce that did not protest.

In addition, there is no doubt that the peoples of the Soviet Union both responded to Stalin's call to defend the Motherland against foreign invaders because of patriotism, and understood that the workplace was a key battlefield.

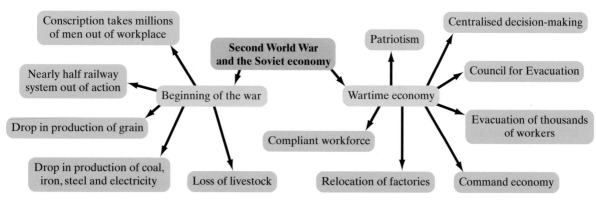

The economic impact of the Second World War on the USSR

Essential notes

Soldiers knew that retreat and surrender could both be punished by execution. Prisoners returning to the USSR after the war were indeed treated as traitors and having left a German POW camp were often sent straight to a Soviet labour camp.

Essential notes

Easing persecution of the Orthodox Church was another factor that kept many Russians fighting. Churches were allowed to reopen and the Orthodox leader announced that it was a 'holy war' against Germany.

Reasons for Soviet victory

Soviet Union's strengths

The Soviet Union defeated Germany because of a number of factors. Vitally, the USSR had four strengths:

1. The mineral wealth of the country was vast.

2. The size of the country made it practically unconquerable.

3. The climate had defeated previous invaders and Russians joked about being defended by 'General Winter'.

4. The population was three times larger than that of Germany.

Balance of forces

The greater population meant that despite the appalling casualty rate, the Soviet Union could endlessly call up new recruits and form new armies in a way that became impossible for the Germans. This meant that the Soviets' loss of more than one million soldiers in the Battle of Stalingrad was less devastating to them than the Germans' loss of 200 000. At the Battle of Kursk, 1.3 million Soviet troops outnumbered the Germans nearly 2:1.

Stalin took no account of Soviet losses and the population itself had been taught to expect no compassion. Hardened by purges, collectivisation, *dekulakisation* and industrialisation, those at the front and those at home knew there would be huge losses. The Great Terror meant that the structures of brutal discipline were already in place. The NKVD played the same role in war as it had in peace. Retreat and surrender would be as fatal for soldiers and their families as disagreement or reluctance had been to peasants and workers.

Stalin's leadership

After he had recovered from the shock of Nazi invasion, Stalin's leadership and decisions were integral to the USSR's victory:

- Five-Year Plans had already put the USSR on a war footing

- wartime reorganisation of the economy

- propaganda emphasis on patriotism and defence of the homeland

- reversal of policy of repression towards the military elite.

Pre-war organisation of the economy

Key to success in the war was pre-war industrialisation. There had been inefficiency, injustice, corruption and judicial murder. Nevertheless, by the time of the 1941 outbreak of war, the USSR had been turned into one of the world's foremost industrial powers, even surpassing Germany in industrial output. Stalin's peacetime decision to prioritise heavy industry and military spending meant the economic plan did not need extensive rewriting to match wartime conditions.

Wartime reorganisation of the economy

Stalin's decision to move whole factories and their workers east of the Urals prevented defence-related industries (such as aircraft factories and steel works) from falling into the hands of the German army. By 1943, the Soviet Union had recovered from the 1941 loss of industrial capacity; factories were in full production. Production of armaments began to outstrip that of Germany, allowing Russian troops to be resupplied more quickly and more fully than the Germans could match.

Patriotism and propaganda

When, on 3 July 1941, Stalin finally addressed the Soviet people, he implored them to fight for the Motherland. Historians draw attention to the fact that in this, the most important speech of his life, he made no mention of the Communist Party or of Marxist ideology. He was appealing to his people as a Russian patriot and as a fellow citizen. The opening words speak for themselves: 'Comrades, citizens, brothers and sisters, men of our Army and Navy! My words are addressed to you, dear friends!' Stalin was able to draw on their patriotism but also the years of the personality cult: he was one of the people and he was asking for the people's help.

Military leadership

In a change of policy, Stalin released thousands of officers, including generals, who had been imprisoned during the purges. Their military expertise was vital, and they went to the front to lead troops. Tsarist-era practices abolished by the Bolsheviks were reintroduced:

- officers received better rations than men
- officers' families received privileged treatment
- military personnel saluted their superiors.

In a key difference from Hitler, Stalin gave his generals control over decision-making. This was a major change of approach from before the war. Historian Geoffrey Roberts argues that as the war went on, Stalin got better at taking advice and the quality of the advice the generals gave him also improved as they learned from experience. Marshal Georgy Zhukov was perhaps the most important military commander on any front in the Second World War.

It is difficult for British students, brought up on the significance of Western victories and defeats, to appreciate the importance of the Eastern Front. In fact, many historians would argue that the key battles of the Second World War were those fought by the Red Army. Zhukov was the chief of the Soviet General Staff and the army's key strategist, directing or involved in all the most significant arenas of the war: the Defence of Moscow, the Siege of Leningrad and the Battles of Stalingrad, Kursk and Berlin.

Examiners' notes

Examiners do not expect you to be able to reel off endless statistics. However, they will want you to show that you understand what was taking place in the economy, can comment on its significance and show its relevance to the question you are answering.

Essential notes

Several historians quote the slogan 'For the Motherland and for Stalin', declaring it something troops shouted on their way into battle. Others disagree and regard it as a story invented by propagandists.

Essential notes

Stalin and Beria were both envious of Zhukov's achievements. After the war he survived several dismissals, demotions and accusations of corruption.

Lend-lease

The Soviets were not left on their own. Under a system called 'lend-lease' established under US President Franklin D. Roosevelt, they received support from countries such as the UK, Canada and especially the USA. Armaments were vital for the fight, but in addition to weapons came supplies to rescue agriculture, support the population and prevent famine, including vast quantities of food, aircraft, tanks, boots, locomotives, lorries, tyres, cotton and woollen fabric.

Stalin remained suspicious of lend-lease throughout the war, not least because the contrast between the higher-quality Western goods and those produced in the Soviet Union was noticed by the Russians themselves. This undermined the propaganda message of Soviet superiority on all fronts. As a result, praising the foreign-made goods could lead to arrest.

Soviet-era statistics play down the importance of lend-lease and suggest that the percentage contribution to industrial production and military *matériel* was small: *Gosplan* declared that the scheme accounted for 4 per cent of those goods used by the Red Army during the Great Patriotic War. On the other hand we know that the scheme provided 95 per cent of the trains by which the Soviet forces were able to travel.

The undeniable fact is that the supply allowed Soviet industry to continue making armaments, as well as helping clothe the army and feed the population. It made a major strategic contribution to the Soviet victory.

Hitler's misjudgements

Nazi racism

The USSR was inhabited by many different peoples with different languages, religions, cultures and traditions. Such diversity might have been a source of weakness as certain regions, such as Ukraine, welcomed the Nazis as liberators, and there was collaboration as well as resistance. However, Nazi racial policies prevented the Germans from making use of anti-Soviet, anti-Stalin and anti-Russian sentiments in Ukraine and elsewhere.

Hitler had defined all Slavs (which included Ukrainians) as *Untermenschen*: sub-human. They could work as slaves but they could not expect treatment appropriate to human beings.

In addition, the Germans were desperate to feed their vast army and pay for their vast war. Accordingly the local people found that the forcible requisitioning of grain continued, only the quotas demanded by the Nazis were higher than those under the Soviets.

It is conceivable that by dividing the non-Russian nationalities from the Russian majority, Germany might have secured the support of the occupied. That would have made occupation easier to maintain and created national disunity. Stalin could not have led a disunited country to victory.

German economic priorities

Hitler believed that the First World War had been lost in part on the home front: the population had stopped supporting the soldiers. He insisted that living standards be maintained and domestic needs satisfied by German industry and agriculture in order to retain popular support for the war. This contrasts strongly with the Soviet's 'all for the Front' approach, which had been made possible in part by the years of social discipline.

Tactical errors

Hitler ordered troops to defend territory regardless of its tactical significance because of the propaganda value of occupying large swathes of Russia. In addition, he opted for besieging Moscow and Leningrad instead of launching an all-out assault.

The sieges tied down large numbers of German troops and *matériel*. The invading armies were then trapped as the weather turned against them. This went completely against the philosophy of *Blitzkrieg*, with rapid advance and low-cost victories. Finally, Hitler insisted both on pushing troops north to Leningrad and north-east to Moscow to capture the major cities, while also directing them south-east to overrun Ukraine and pushing on to the Caspian to capture grain and oil supplies. This spread his forces over a vast front running from the Baltic to the Black Sea.

Poor timing and the weather

Some historians suggest that Hitler had delayed the invasion of the Soviet Union by two months to allow his army to complete the Balkans Campaign. Had he invaded two months earlier, the initial successes would have been easier to follow up as his armies would have had a longer period of good weather in which to fight. This would have allowed the campaign to be shorter and thus more like the earlier successes on the Western Front.

As it was, once the initial *Blitzkrieg* had slowed, his armies were caught up in a long campaign running into an unseasonably wet autumn in 1941 and then one of the coldest winters in living memory. Supplies were unable to keep pace with the changing conditions and German soldiers lacked appropriate clothing for the Russian winter. As the German advance halted, the Soviets were given time to recover and Zhukov was able to plan and launch a counter-offensive.

Reasons for Soviet victory: a summary

The Great Patriotic War

Examiners' notes

Questions on the reasons for Soviet victory require you to show understanding of mistakes made by the Germans. Examiners are not testing you on 'Hitler's Germany 1933–45'; your topic is Stalin's Russia 1924–53. However, contrasting aspects of Soviet strength with Nazi weakness will be credited.

Emergence of the Soviet Union as a superpower

Grand Alliance

Stalin emerged from the war as leader of one of the world's two most powerful countries. Yet he did not win the war on his own. He was part of a Grand Alliance between the USA, Great Britain and the USSR.

Together, the three faced a common enemy in Nazi Germany, but theirs was always a strained alliance. Democracy and communism were different, with conflicting political ideologies, and neither side trusted each other. At the end of the war, with no common enemy to fight against, the alliance disintegrated. Europe divided along lines agreed during the war into two groups of nations.

Spheres of influence

Even while the war was still being fought, the allies had planned the post-war settlement:

Date	Event	Significant decisions
1941	Atlantic Charter	UK and the USA agree not to seek territorial expansion in the war, aggressors should be disarmed, peoples should have right to self-determination
1943	Tehran Conference	German–Polish border set
1944	Secret meeting between Churchill and Stalin	Outlines post-war 'spheres of influence'
1945 (February)	Yalta Conference	Austria and Germany to be divided into zones of occupation; Germany demilitarised and de-Nazified; elections to take place in Eastern Europe; Russian–Polish borders set; UN founded
1945 (July–August)	Potsdam Conference (post-war)	Draws up the post-war map of Europe

The post-war settlement

Building an empire

At the end of the war the USSR extended its influence into eastern and central Europe. The 11-million-strong Red Army had occupied most of this area by the end of the European war in May 1945. During the war, the Allies had held a series of meetings and conferences (see the table above). At these they had discussed national self-determination, settled the post-war borders of Europe but also agreed that there would be 'spheres of influence'.

Economic power

The Soviet Union's superpower status was supported by its economy. In 1945, the USSR showed the impact of the years of fighting. Huge numbers of towns, farms and factories had been destroyed. The infrastructure of roads, bridges, railways and electrical supply had been badly damaged. There was a vast homelessness problem and the casualties among both military and civilians had left a drastic shortage of labour. To make matters worse, 1946 saw a poor harvest because of unusually dry weather.

Despite this, Stalin announced that the country had to set the goal of becoming the world's leading economy within 15 years. He failed to agree loans with the USA, but succeeded in being granted reparation payments from the defeated Germany; much of this was taken in the form of entire industrial installations being relocated to the USSR on the model of the wartime evacuation. This allowed the Soviet Union to develop new weaponry, keeping pace with the wealthier West. In addition, the client states signed trade agreements that favoured the USSR.

Fourth Five-Year Plan

Stalin's priority during the first three Five-Year Plans had been defence. While this distorted the economy, the emphasis on the military had benefited the Soviet Union during the war. Even with the war over, military expenditure and heavy industry continued to take precedence over consumer industries. In the Fourth Five-Year Plan, spending on the armed forces was half as large again as it had been before the war.

Output rose dramatically for coal, electricity and steel, yet the standard of living for its citizens continued to suffer. Housing was inadequate in both number and quality: a poor housing situation had been worsened by the retreating Germans, who routinely burned or blew up entire villages and towns, as well as destroying bridges, industry and power stations.

Military power

In the post-war world, the Soviet Union rivalled the USA in the production of conventional weapons. By 1949, the Soviet atomic programme headed by Igor Kurchatov broke the American nuclear monopoly, for the following reasons:

- Access to necessary raw materials: East Germany and Czechoslovakia had deposits of uranium.
- Command economy: central planning agencies could divert resources to the development of nuclear weapons.
- Spies: Klaus Fuchs, Ted Hall and others passed the West's nuclear secrets to the Russians.
- Beria: the secret police ran the programme, giving participants a mixture of protection and fear.

After 1949, the arms race between the USA and the Soviet Union began.

Soviet power

In 1939, the Soviet Union had been isolated and unable to create the alliances it sought. By the time of Stalin's death, it was a member of the security council of the United Nations, a nuclear power and the dominant power in a powerful military alliance, which in 1955 would become the Warsaw Pact.

Yet the purges continued: at the time of the 1952 19th Party Congress, Beria and Molotov were convinced they were in danger. There was no press or artistic freedom. There was no opportunity to show initiative. However much had changed, more change still lay in the future.

Essential notes

The Fifth Five-Year Plan (1951–5) prioritised defence, heavy industry and reconstruction. Agriculture was set targets but there was little attempt either to make them realistic or to achieve them. By 1952 industrial production was nearly double 1941 figures, while agricultural production had barely returned to 1940 levels.

Essential notes

Despite continuing problems, food rationing had ended in 1947.

Essential notes

Igor Kurchatov began his research into the atomic bomb in the early 1940s and was the director of the Soviet nuclear programme. He worked with Georgy Flyorov and Andrei Sakharov.

Essential notes

Klaus Fuchs was a refugee from the Nazis. Ted Hall was an American nuclear physicist. Both worked on nuclear research in America's Manhattan Project. Both passed American nuclear secrets to the Soviets, believing that such weapons belonging to one side only was unfair and unsafe.

Introduction

This section of the book covers the skills you must use to gain a high grade. Although you need to have learned and understood the content of your course, you will not get many marks for simply repeating what you know. Questions always have a specific focus and you need to be able to identify this, select the best and most useful evidence and then apply it in a suitable way. This guidance should help you do this better.

The sections below will:

• show you how to interpret what a question is asking for

• help you decide which question will be your strongest

• show you how to structure and write your answer

• explain how the mark scheme works

• give some advice on how to plan your revision effectively.

The Unit 1 exam is based on Assessment Objective 1. It tests your ability to select relevant historical knowledge from what you have learned and to use it to support an argument that leads to a judgement based on the question you are tackling. The guidance given here will help you develop these skills.

In the exam, you will have 1 hour and 20 minutes to write two essays. You will answer one question on each of your two topics. These notes cover D4, Stalin's Russia 1924–53.

Working out the focus of the question

Understanding the words in the question

Always read the questions very carefully because each one has been put together to give you clues about how to answer it. Note any phrases used in the title and do not attempt a question unless you know what you are being asked to do.

Here is an explanation of the most common words and phrases that you will see. Make sure you know what they mean.

Question wording	Definition
Responsible for	Causing to happen
Significant	Important
Outcome	Result
Course	The unfolding of events
Nature	What something is like
Turning point	An event, after which things changed
Key features	The most important aspects
Transformation	Change of such significance that the whole nature of something is altered
Modernisation	Bringing up to date
Undergo	Experience

You will also be expected to know certain specialist historical terms that may come up in the question. Make sure you know what these mean.

Word	Definition
Dictatorship	A political system where power lies in the hands of a single person
Totalitarian	A political system where a dictator exercises complete power over all aspects of life
Bolsheviks	Lenin's faction within the Social Democrats, which successfully seized power in November 1917 and ruled Russia afterwards
Revolution	An event, or series of events, possibly violent, resulting in significant political, social or economic change
Repression	The use of harsh measures to keep control of people
The Great Terror	The period of particularly harsh repression of suspected traitors in the mid-1930s, following the death of Kirov
Purges	Literally, internal cleansing. In the 1930s, the wave of arrests and executions of suspected traitors inside the Communist Party
Soviet	The Russian word for council – can be local or national. Eventually came to mean the same as 'communist'
Coup	Seizing of power, usually by force
Collectivisation (of agriculture)	The process by which peasants were forced to live in government-run farms where everything was communally owned
NEP	New Economic Policy 1921–7 that restored some capitalist practices to the countryside to get peasants producing more food
Kulaks	Better-off peasants who had done well out of NEP and were then targeted as enemies of communism
Five-Year Plans	The central planning schemes to accelerate industrialisation involving strict control and target setting
Show Trials	The rigged trials of alleged traitors given maximum media exposure
War Economy	Adapting the economy to give priority to war materials rather than consumer goods
Culture	A wide term covering all areas of the arts and media, through which communist ideology was promoted

There are further additional specialist terms that you are likely to need in constructing your answer. In the revision checklist section on pages 98–9 you will find a checklist that will start you off with terms and names that may prove useful.

Recognising the different types of question

Once you have seen a few past questions it will become obvious that there are certain types of question that are often set. You can break them down into three main types.

Questions focusing on causation

- Causation questions with a stated factor, in which you are asked to assess the importance of a stated factor alongside that of other factors.
- Causation questions asking 'why', without any stated factor, in which you are asked to explain the various reasons why something occurred and the links between them.

Questions focusing on change

- Assessing the extent of change
- Assessing the nature of change

Questions focusing on consequences

- Identifying and explaining the results, outcomes, consequences or impact of something on something else.
- Assessing the significance of something and explaining why it is important.

These are not watertight categories. There will be some overlap within each of the three types. It is important that you can recognise which type of question you are doing so that you can structure your answer to tackle it directly. This applies particularly to 'consequence' questions. A common mistake is to start explaining the *causes* of a situation when you should actually be *assessing its consequences*. Below, each of these three types is examined in more detail.

Causation questions with a stated factor

This is the commonest type of question you will see.

General points

To answer these questions, you need to weigh up the significance of the stated factor, alongside that of other factors that you must work out for yourself. It makes sense to start with the stated factor, then to broaden your response to deal with the others. You must make sure you address both in order to get a secure level 4 mark or above (see the explanation of the mark scheme, pages 93–5).

Sum up the significance of each factor you have discussed and comment on its relative importance. This will help to clarify your thoughts about the judgement that you need to make in the conclusion.

Planned example

'How accurate is it to say that Stalin's success in the power struggle was mainly due to the power he held inside the Communist Party?'

In the introduction make it clear that you realise that without the influential positions Stalin held inside the party, it would have been very difficult for him to have won the struggle; however, since there was a range of wider factors operating as well. Identify these other factors (do not just say there were other factors) but resist the temptation to go into detail about them here: his central position on key ideological issues; the value of his moderate image standing above the most vicious in-fighting; the narrower support base of the other contenders; key tactical errors made by some of the others, particularly Trotsky, but to a lesser extent Zinoviev and Kamenev; Stalin's ability to exploit circumstances in order to discredit the views held by others.

You may well find extra ones or break them down in a slightly different way but you will not have time to cover all the contributory factors because the list is potentially very long.

As far as the stated factor is concerned, identify the key posts Stalin held and show you understand that having this party influence was vital because he could ensure crucial votes went in his favour.

Also show you understand that the time frame covers the period from Lenin's death (even just before, if you like) up to the vote in the 1929 Party Congress and their decision to remove the right-wing opposition from their posts.

Ideally, you should indicate how you will be arguing your case – whether you are putting most emphasis on the stated factor or one of the others. At this stage, you may want to keep your options open in the introduction. Make sure your argument is clear, though, by the time you reach the conclusion.

The main section should be a series of paragraphs devoted to each factor in turn, starting with the stated one of Stalin's party powers.

For each factor, make a point, provide detailed supporting evidence and explain its relevance to Stalin's victory – then you will be answering the question directly. The table overleaf shows how you might go about it, but you will need to expand on the material in the *supporting evidence* column to ensure your point is well covered.

You may well decide that the stated factor deserves more than one paragraph, since you are never going to be given a stated factor that is not significant.

Remember:

- indicate how you intend to argue your case in the introduction
- reach a clear judgement in your conclusion.

In each paragraph think **PEER:**

- Point
- Evidence
- Explained Relevance to the question

Point	Supporting evidence	Explanation of relevance
Stated factor (1) Power that came from being Party Secretary (combined with having a *Politburo* seat)	He could control *Politburo* agenda, appoint supporters as regional and local party secretaries, select delegates to attend annual Congress, supervise recruitment under the Lenin Enrolment (1924–5) and expel troublemakers from Communist Party	Because Party Congress had power to take key policy decisions and vote for members of Central Committee – by packing it with his supporters Stalin got approval to abandon NEP in 1928 and Right Opposition dismissed from posts in 1929 Because membership of Communist Party doubled under Lenin Enrolment and these new members sought to further careers by showing loyalty to Stalin Because local secretaries could control voting in their areas and they too owed their positions to Stalin
Stated factor (2) Contrast above with limited powers of the other contenders	Trotsky – only had support in Red Army and among young radicals on far left Zinoviev – only as Leningrad Communist Party leader Kamenev – only as Moscow Communist Party chief Bukharin – had no real base, just general popularity, especially with younger generation	Trotsky's support base socially limited, Kamenev's and Zinoviev's geographically Popularity did not necessarily mean power – none could control outcomes of meetings as Stalin could
Other factor (1) Stalin's central position on key ideological issues – speed of industrialisation, exporting the revolution, nature of leadership	Stalin advocated retaining NEP for practical reasons only as long as it was working; focusing on 'socialism in one country' rather than 'permanent revolution' for the time being, again for pragmatic reasons; and appeared to agree with collective leadership until he broke with the Right in 1929	Because this enabled him to make tactical adjustments without appearing contradictory (unlike those to his left and right whose stances were determined more by ideological conviction than practical realities of what was best for Russia at any time); also because occupying central ground gave more scope for broadening support than being on extremes, so contrast with left-wing views of Trotsky, Zinoviev and Kamenev and right-wing views of Bukharin which made expansion of their appeal more difficult
Other factor (2) Value of Stalin's moderate image	For years he was seen more as a dedicated administrator who took on dull jobs, than a potential leader ('Comrade Card Index', the 'grey blur', etc.); he also left in-fighting to Zinoviev, Kamenev and Trotsky while he appeared to stand above it, even appealing for unity	Because this enabled him to build up power quietly without appearing a threat. Clear contrast with Trotsky who many feared as a potential dictator – a 'Russian Bonaparte'

Point	Supporting evidence	Explanation of relevance
Other factor (3) Stalin's sense of timing and ability to exploit changing circumstances	Stalin skilful at creating alliances but broke them and shifted allegiance when circumstances were advantageous, e.g. 1925 advocating socialism in one country (and continuing NEP) won right-wing support and isolated Zinoviev, Kamenev and Trotsky. For example, 1928 grain procurement problems justified ending NEP and defending Russia from growing external hostility by industrialising faster for military reasons	Needs linking with Stalin's ability to pack crucial Congress meetings and centrality of his stance. Because Stalin was clever at sensing best time to change tack, but only he had power to control outcomes of Congress meetings that took key decisions, so value of this factor dependent on stated factor
Other factor (4) Errors made by others (that Stalin exploited)	Trotsky missed Lenin's funeral; alienated others by his writing and general arrogance, making no effort to cultivate support Kamenev lacked leadership qualities and judgement – 'New Opposition' with Zinoviev and Trotsky was ill-advised Zinoviev was personally unpopular and also joined 'New Opposition' All underestimated Stalin	Trotsky laid himself open to accusations of disloyalty and personal ambition. Zinoviev and Kamenev were tainted by association with Trotsky (despite having opposed him initially). Stress it was Stalin's ability to exploit these mistakes that made them important – also by creating the Lenin cult he could exaggerate impressions of disloyalty by recalling old disputes (though this could also work against him)
Other factor (5) Luck	All leaders wanted to suppress Lenin's testament; Trotsky often ill and absent from Moscow	Stalin would have come out worst from Lenin's *Testament* so suppression suited him best – link to Trotsky's errors since he failed to push for its publication. Plotting against Trotsky easier if he was not physically present

In your conclusion you need to reach a clear judgement about the relative importance of the above factors and why you see it the way you do. If you have put the stress on the stated factor as the main reason, reiterate why you see the powers Stalin held inside the Communist Party as essential to his victory and which element of these powers you see as most important. It is good if you can comment on how he used these powers at specific times to win crucial votes as well as building them up slowly behind the scenes in the earlier years.

Remember to highlight the links between the factors you have discussed because Stalin also needed to be able to discredit other people and their ideas, so their mistakes came into play. He would not have built up these powers without having personal qualities of his own.

Causation questions asking 'why?', without any stated factor

General points

These questions may look very straightforward but can be deceptive. They usually include a twist of some kind, such as asking 'Why, despite x, did a certain outcome result?' or 'Why did a certain development occur at a certain time?'

It is important to group your reasons logically and to give each one appropriate weighting according to its significance. Remember to keep linking your reason back to the focus of the question. Avoid producing an answer that reads like a list of potential reasons with little comment on the significance of each one.

Make sure your judgement is explicitly stated in the conclusion.

Planned example

'Why, despite his victory in the power struggle by 1929, did Stalin increase the level of Terror in the 1930s?'

This particular question is asking you to explain why the 'normal' level of terror became the so-called 'Great Terror'. Key things to cover will be:

- Why did it continue at all, once the succession to Lenin had been sorted out?

- Why did it become more intense at this particular time?

The murder of Kirov in 1934 is generally regarded as being of central importance to any explanation of the purges, but the wider explanations need to be examined as well. You need to link it to the economic, as well as political and personal contexts.

In your introduction, show you are aware that there is a debate about the exact reasons why Terror reached such heights because the reasons are complicated and inter-linked. The peak period was 1936–8 so if you say it was only after this that Stalin could feel really secure you have taken on board the extra twist in the question. Identify the range of possible explanations that you could categorise as political, economic and personal to make them more manageable. Indicate where you think the emphasis should be placed. A very plausible approach would be to argue that the emergence of Kirov as a popular alternative Secretary-General at the 1934 Congress was likely to have been the factor that caused the escalation from 'normal' levels of communist terror to these unprecedented heights.

In the main section each paragraph must explain a relevant reason. It would make sense to group your explanations along the lines suggested here.

Type of reason	Supporting evidence	Explanation of relevance
Political	1932 Ryutin Affair 1934 Congress – support for Kirov as 'alternative Secretary' 'Old' Bolsheviks knew too much about Stalin Fear of military coup Fear of Germany after 1933	Ryutin's criticisms showed Stalin not in complete control, re-emphasised by Kirov's popularity Convenient opportunity to remove the likes of Kamenev, Zinoviev and Bukharin in Show Trials Red Army an alternative centre of power – old fear of military dictator (Bonaparte … Trotsky?) Likelihood of future war with Germany in view of Hitler's views – would require unity in Russia so critics had to be eradicated in advance
Economic	Ryutin's call for fresh start; Kirov's criticisms of breakneck pace of change; mistakes of First FYP; lack of consumer goods; brutality of forced collectivisation Growth of *gulags* as pool of slave labour Statistics	Because earliest Show Trials targeted economic critics (Menshevik Trial 1932) this suggests Stalin was expecting criticism of new economic policies and was taking pre-emptive action to create fear and head it off Links to political challenges of moderates favouring slowdown after problems of First FYP and scale of *kulak* opposition New industrial projects required labour – *gulags* supplied it, especially for most unpleasant tasks, e.g. building White Sea Canal
Personal	Kirov was a possible challenger to Stalin Role of Yezhov in widening Terror to all areas of society	New generation of communists bound to challenge at some point – Stalin must have expected to be challenged Yezhov feeding Stalin's paranoia to avoid same fate as Yagoda, so widened Terror to prove his loyalty
Others	It developed a momentum of its own due to climate of fear. Terror from below as well as above	People informed on each other for self-advancement or protection

In your conclusion you need to sum up the importance of these factors and make it clear why you see your main factor as the most influential in raising terror from its normal level to the very high levels of the 'Yezhovshchina'. You can reiterate that there is still some debate over the exact causes (was it 'top down' from Stalin or 'bottom up' from the grass roots, or a mixture of the two?) and that the three strands above are impossible to separate.

Change questions: assessing the extent of change

General points

Extent of change questions require you to work out how much certain things changed over a specified time period and identify things that hardly changed at all. Nature of change questions will ask you to assess whether there was progress or modernisation, whether something grew stronger or weaker, and so on. In either type of question you need to establish the criteria on which you will be basing your judgements, depending on how the question is worded: your judgement could be based on the numbers of people affected by the change or the length of time the change lasted or took to implement. It will depend on the individual question. Comparing the state of affairs before and after the event in question can be a useful way of working out the extent and significance of the changes.

Try to show awareness of the more subtle differences depending on what is being discussed. Avoid bland comments such as 'politics changed a lot/ hardly at all', and so on. Break things down so you can make more telling comments and contrast the rates of change in different areas or at different times in the given period.

Planned example

'How successful was the Communist Party in transforming the Russian economy 1928–41?'

In your introduction, establish the criteria on which you are going to base your judgement of 'success', so first decide what the Communist Party were aiming to achieve in terms of 'transforming the economy'. In economic terms they wanted to industrialise much more rapidly in order to rearm and protect Russia from its external enemies; and to shake up agriculture so that it produced enough to feed the cities and to sell abroad to buy industrial machinery. You will also need to make it clear that you understand what 'transformation' means – not just change, but change beyond recognition. Your line of argument should be indicated, for example, there was a transformation in terms of how industry and agriculture were organised, but changes in overall production were much more variable.

In your main section, you should clearly differentiate between areas that changed drastically enough to merit 'transformation' and those where less significant change occurred.

Aim	Transformation	Less significant change
Make agriculture more productive	By 1936 practically all farms collectivised. This released labour to cities, or *gulags* Food supplies to cities and exports enabled FYPs to progress (see below) Farming techniques modernised – mechanisation and scientific methods spread	Patchy progress depending on date – peasant repossessions after 'Dizzy with success' 1930, then resumption of coercion. Differences between *soukhoz* (entirely state owned) and *kolkhoz* (where small private plots retained, so element of compromise) Food production down at first, leading to famine 1932; 1939 production only up to 1913 level Scientific progress slow to spread
Industrialise at full pace (and defend Russia from enemies)	Central planning under *Gosplan*, which set detailed targets of FYPs. Creation of a command economy Huge projects – Dnieper Dam, Stalingrad Tractor Plant and Magnitogorsk Steel Works Impressive production figures for coal, oil, steel, electricity. Economic growth 1928–32 while capitalist world in Depression New working practices – Stakhanovite movement, shock brigades, etc. Rearmament under the Second and Third FYPs – later war economy based on this. Eastern relocation of strategic industries	Production figures misleading: plenty of workers but mainly unskilled, poor quality of goods and unreliable statistics. There was a fear and culture of dishonesty. Significant under achieving areas – chemicals at first, consumer goods most of time. Negative impact of purges of experts

In your conclusion you can reinforce your judgement by restating areas where 'transformation' is an appropriate term for the changes brought in – the adoption of the collective farming system and the introduction of a command economy where production of some goods reached impressive levels – while acknowledging the areas where changes were less dramatic than they might appear.

Change questions: assessing the nature of change
General points
For these questions, you need to discuss the nature of change (whether there was progress or modernisation, whether something grew stronger or weaker and so on).

Planned example
For an example of a nature of change question, refer to the mind map on page 85.

Consequence questions: assessing the impact

General points

These questions require you to explain the impact of something on something else. The wording may vary between consequences, effects, results, outcome, and so on, but the question still wants you to focus on what happened because of another event. You should focus on the stated factor's impact, but do not confine your answer to this – you should also discuss other relevant factors that caused an impact.

It can be useful to divide your response into short- and long-term impact, since effects vary as time passes. For example, the first big Show Trial, that of 'the 16' in 1936 had a far greater impact than that of the third, the 'Trial of the 21' in 1938 because people gradually became sceptical and hardened. However, in other examples you might wish to show that the cumulative effect of things can build up over time, until it takes a comparatively minor trigger to set off a major consequence.

Planned example

'How far can the USSR's ability to resist German invasion 1941–3 be seen as a consequence of Stalin's economic policies of the 1930s?'

In your introduction you will need to state clearly that the USSR's ability to resist the invasion was partly due to the economic policies of the 1930s, so identify their consequences here (rearmament, establishment of a central planning infrastructure, downgrading of consumer goods, use of women in the workforce, relocation of industries to east, and so on). Then indicate the other reasons that also help explain their ability to resist (lend-lease, the strength of inherent Russian nationalism, German mistakes, and so on). Make your line of argument clear – it was surely due to a combination of the economic policies plus some additional factors that you should identify here if you have already decided.

In the main section, deal first with the stated factor of Stalin's economic policies of the 1930s, and then with the other factors that enabled Russia to survive.

In your conclusion make sure you have reached a judgement about the extent to which the 1930s economic policies impacted on Russia's capacity to resist the Germans. Restate the most important aspects of these policies that helped in the war but also put them in perspective by weighing them against the most important of your 'additional' factors. You might want to consider the different interpretations – the old Soviet view that emphasises the successful nature of the economic policies in defeating a capitalist invader (and of course downplaying the value of lend-lease) and the Western liberal view, which prefers to see Russia resisting the Germans despite the economic policies of the 1930s.

General factor	More specific aspect	Impact on ability to resist 1941–3
1930s economic policies	Production of war materials a feature of all FYPs and top priority of Third.	Meant heavy industrial base on which arms production depended already in place and enabled Russia to outproduce Germany in weapons, tanks and planes by 1943. Russia spent greater proportion of national income on war goods than any other country
	Central planning machinery already in place	War did not necessitate new organisation of economy – *Gosplan's* existing expertise could be applied in wartime to direct production to military purposes.
	Workforce already regimented and hardened by long hours and lack of consumer goods	Meant wartime privations were no shock. People were used to rationing and queuing *Gulag* system already in place to keep factories supplied with labour at low cost
	Female workforce had expanded by 10 million in 1930s	Meant it was easy to continue the trend as more men conscripted and to conscript women as well. Contrast this with German reluctance to conscript women
	Relocation of thousands of industries and millions of people to east	Put key industries beyond the reach of the invading German forces and allowed them to keep producing
Additional factors	Stalin's decision to remain in Moscow for duration of war	Lifted morale of soldiers and civilians, since safety of Moscow in doubt 1941–2
	Availability of vital raw materials through lend-lease from 1941 helped offset consequences of losing so much of western Russia to invaders	Aluminium and copper essential for arms industry and coal supplies compensated for loss of Donbass region to Germans. Tinned food (Spam) allowed Russians to continue to focus on war goods rather than consumer goods. Communications systems could still function due to provision of radio equipment, rail stock, jeeps and trucks
	Russian nationalism remained strong and outweighed resentment at pre-war suffering. Early pro-German feelings soon vanished as Nazi racism became obvious – Russian propaganda had plenty to build on	Pre-war propaganda had already been stirring up anti-German feelings and this was stepped up in wartime by, for example, Shostakovich's 'Leningrad Symphony'. War depicted as 'Great Patriotic War' in defence of the 'Motherland'
	Easing persecution of Church	Lifted public morale to find solace in religion. Church leaders supported government in return (Note: only really began in 1943 so maybe more important later)
	German military errors helped Russians: • launching Barbarossa so late in year • switching focus of attack to Stalingrad instead of focusing on Moscow • refusal to retreat from Stalingrad	 Over-optimistic to think conquest could be completed in late summer 1942 Attack on Stalingrad left Germans too stretched further north but Moscow more important Led to capture of German Sixth Army
	Other specific military successes for Russians: • scorched earth retreat • resistance of Leningrad • Battle of Kursk	 Retreat denied Germans resources and caused them huge problems over winters Leningrad's survival inspired rest of country – symbolic of heroic resistance Victory finished off Germans and accelerated their retreat after Stalingrad

Consequence questions: assessing the significance

General points

Here you are being asked to weigh up the way a specified factor impacted on something else. It is important to focus on the stated factor since you will not be asked to assess the significance of something unimportant. However, you might broaden your answer to discuss other factors that had an impact.

Planned example

'How far do you agree that the collectivisation of agriculture was a catastrophe for the Russian people 1928–39?'

In your introduction, show you know that collectivisation resulted in terrible suffering for large numbers of people due to the famine it caused and the disruption of the lives of the thousands sent to *gulags,* so for huge numbers 'catastrophe' is not an exaggeration. You do not need to write out a definition of 'catastrophe', but you need to be aware what it means. However, you will also need to identify the positives that came out of it (urban workers got reliable food supplies, FYPs could go ahead) and reach a judgement about whether these outweighed the obvious negatives as far as the 'Russian people' were concerned. Ultimately your judgement will depend on which sections of the 'Russian people' were most affected and whether the significance changed as things settled down again.

Divide the main section into two parts – first examining the 'catastrophic' results, then looking at who may have benefited.

Catastrophic	Beneficial
In terms of loss of life and human suffering, due to: speed of change; peasant resistance and destruction of food resources, leading to huge fall in grain yields and livestock numbers, which in turn lead to famine, especially bad in Ukraine. Possibly 10 million deaths in early 1930s	In terms of allowing the FYPs to progress
	Possible to argue that future security of Russian people ultimately depended on their success because Russia was able to protect itself from foreign enemies
Decision to 'liquidate *kulaks*' (1929) directly catastrophic for them (executions, *gulags*) and indirectly made overall situation worse by removing most enterprising farmers. Food production levels still below 1913 level in 1935	Urban workers ensured adequate food supplies (even though rationing frequent, so never in plentiful amounts)
	Food exported to buy industrial machinery on which FYPs initially depended
Destruction of thousands of families also catastrophic – permanently split up by disruption that collectivisation involved	Helped secure communist control of the people, so beneficial to party leaders, Stalin in particular

In your conclusion, restate why you see the impact as you do. Make your judgement based on an assessment of the various consequences of collectivisation over the decade that followed its implementation.

Choosing the best question to tackle

Once you understand the differences between these three question types, it should be much easier for you to choose the best question to tackle. If you can recognise the question types, you should be able to construct quick outline plans based on the examples given in the preceding pages.

For example, for the question 'How far do you agree that Stalin's policies in the 1930s restored Russian society to its traditional values?' you should be able to work out that this is a 'nature of change' question and you could plan it with a brief mind map like this:

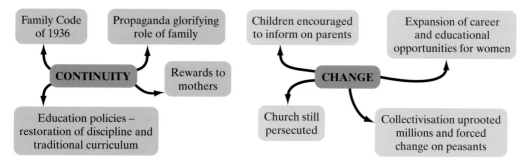

Evidence of return to traditional values and of continued change

Structuring and writing an effective answer

In brief

Essays need to be structured into three sections: the introduction, the main body of the argument and the conclusion. Structuring your answer clearly is really important for two reasons: firstly, it helps the examiner follow your answer so they can give it the mark it deserves and secondly, it helps you keep focused on the question.

1. The introduction is important but should not be too long – five or six lines should be enough. You need to identify the range of factors you intend to discuss in the main section and to give an idea of how you intend to argue your case – the line of argument you intend to develop in the main section. If there are words in the title that need to be explained, then do this here. You also need to show you understand why any particular dates have been selected.

2. The main section should be a series of four to six developed paragraphs that will lead to a substantial conclusion. Start each paragraph with a point that you are making as part of your argument. You need to provide accurate and reasonably precise evidence to support the point and then explain clearly how it adds to your argument. This last requirement is often what students forget to do, so practise making your point explicitly relevant and keep referring back to the wording of the question to remind yourself what the argument is about. Remember to address both sides of the argument, such as continuity and change or the stated factor and the other factors.

3. The conclusion should sum up the points in your argument and make it clear why you are arguing your case in this particular way. Do not suddenly throw in any new ideas at this stage – the conclusion should follow on from what you have already written. It is a good idea to stress what you see as the crucial point in your case and why this is so. It is vital to have a conclusion so the examiner can see the overall judgement you have reached.

In detail

In the section that follows you will see relatively weak examples, followed by revised, stronger examples to illustrate how to structure and write an effective answer.

Introduction

Think about this question and read the responses that follow.

'How far can the USSR's ability to resist German invasion 1941–3 be seen as a consequence of Stalin's economic policies of the 1930s?'

Weak example

Russia survived the German invasion that began in 1941 for several reasons. Stalin's economic policies of the 1930s helped because they had been rearming at top speed during the third Five Year Plan but there were other reasons as well which had little to do with the earlier economic policies. By 1943 the Germans were on the retreat.

This is a reasonable start because it focuses on the question and shows awareness of why these two years have been singled out. It suggests one valid reason why the 1930s economic policies led to successful resistance, but is vague about the other reasons.

Strong example

Russia's ability to resist the Germans in these years was due to a combination of the economic policies of the 1930s and some additional factors. Rearmament had been a feature of all three Five-Year Plans but was the top priority from 1938 onwards, and the development of a planned economy meant that the structure to organise it in wartime was already in place before 1941. However, additional factors also played a part, notably the patriotism of the Russians, the help they got from their allies and the fact that the Germans made crucial errors.

This is much better because, as well as focusing on the question, it gives a clear idea of the main consequences of the 1930s economic policies and identifies three other factors that contributed. The details of the different factors can be unpacked in the main sections. The line of argument is clearer because it says there was a combination of reasons.

Main section

Deal with your most important point in the first paragraph – this will be the stated factor in a multi-factor question or the most significant factor in other types. The basic formula is to support your point with examples from your knowledge and then make it clear how this adds weight to your argument.

Weak example

The most important part of the economic policies of the 1930s was the way they prioritised rearmament after 1938, by moving factories east of the Urals and focusing almost entirely on producing weapons so that there were hardly any consumer goods available to buy. The Russians managed to outproduce the Germans in tanks and aircraft during the war because they had made their preparations beforehand.

While this is a reasonable paragraph, there is little explanation going on here. It fails to say why moving factories east was a good idea, nor does it say why they were able to outproduce the Germans. There is quite a bit of description and not enough explanation.

Strong example

Because rearmament had been a main aim ever since the Five-Year Plans began in 1928, by 1943 the Russians were able to outproduce the Germans in military equipment. Once they had the heavy industrial base in place they could prioritise producing tanks and aircraft in the third plan, and because industries had been relocated in the east they were away from the invading armies and could continue producing. The plans were based on a centralised system in the 1930s, which made it easy to apply this to arms production in wartime. In these two ways the economic policies of the 1930s made wartime production much more straightforward.

What follows is better because the importance of the point about the east is explained and made explicitly relevant to the survival of the Russians. It also explains how centralised planning in peacetime made it easier in wartime. The final comment links both points to the question.

You should follow this approach to each paragraph, addressing a new point each time, and where possible linking back to previous points to show you understand the connections.

In the best essays, one paragraph follows on naturally from the one before. You can do this by starting the new point with a comment that refers back to what is said at the end of the previous paragraph.

For example, after the paragraph on the previous page, you might launch the next one like this to show that the 1930s policies prepared the population for the suffering to come.

> Furthermore, because consumer goods were in short supply for most of the 1930s, people were used to not having them and could endure the hardships of war more easily. They were used to working long hours, seven days a week and knew it was pointless complaining.

It is important to finish each point by linking back to the wording of the title in some way, almost like writing a mini-conclusion at the end of each paragraph. This should guarantee that you are directly addressing the question, which is what you need to be doing to get a mark within level 4 or 5.

So far these sample paragraphs have dealt only with the stated consequence so of course you need to follow a similar approach to paragraphs on the additional factors that were picked out in the introduction. Also, if you are arguing that a consequence other than the stated one was the most important, then your answer should reflect this.

Conclusion

The conclusion should round off all the points you have already made in your argument and make clear why you have argued your case in this particular way. Do not introduce a brand new point at this stage! Reaching a clear judgement is essential for good marks. Emphasise which point has been the most crucial in helping you reach that decision and why you consider it to be so important. If your argument used longer-term and shorter-term factors, go back to these to show that there were different factors operating at different points in time. Refer to any dates in the question here and make sure you are dealing with the whole time period.

If you find you have only five minutes left, and have still not started a conclusion, move straight on to it. You will get more marks this way because the examiner needs to see that you have reached an overall judgement.

Keeping with the same question as on page 87, a reasonable conclusion
might look like this:

Weak example

Therefore, the economic policies of the 1930s
helped the Russians resist the Germans and push
them back towards the west from 1943 onwards.
The economy was geared up for arms production
and the workers were used to being regimented and
suffering hardship even before the war began. While
the allied Lend Lease scheme also helped, along with
the fanatical patriotism and the military mistakes
made by the Germans, it was the Five-Year Plans that
enabled Russia to survive.

This restates the main contributory factors and
reaches a judgement, but it is not really made clear
why this interpretation has been arrived at. The
stated consequence of 1930s economic policies and
the additional factors are both mentioned, but as
separate things.

Strong example

Overall, Russia's ability to resist the Germans would
not have been possible without the economic
changes made in the 1930s. While patriotic fervour,
allied help with food and transport and Germany's
tactical errors did contribute, these factors alone
would not have led to Russia's success. The key
factor was that the Russian economy had already
been industrialised and reorganised in such a
centralised way that adapting it quickly to the
demands of wartime was possible after 1941. Once
the German armies were defeated at Kursk, it was
only a matter of time before the Germans were
completely removed from Russian soil.

This one sums up a clearer judgement by showing
the relative importance of the stated and additional
consequences that have been discussed, as well as
restating the main factors involved.

Key tips

Introducing new paragraphs

- Each paragraph needs to be based on a point in your argument. It will be more convincing if one point leads on to the next, so it is worth practising ways of starting new points that do this. If one point has elements in common with the one before, then show this by using 'In a similar way…'

- Where you are moving to a different kind of point, start with 'In contrast…'

- Sometimes the next point will reinforce the previous one, so try using 'Moreover…' or simply 'In addition…'

- Try starting with 'Nevertheless…' when dealing with a contrasting situation.

- In the course of your paragraph you will need to emphasise the importance of the key points compared to the less important ones, so have a vocabulary at your disposal to help you create a sense of hierarchy. Words such as 'significant', 'major', 'decisive' and 'effective' can do this.

- Words such as 'strong', 'successful' and 'competent' convey much more accurate meaning than 'good'. Likewise, 'weak', 'unsuccessful' and 'incompetent' are much more expressive than 'bad'.

- If you are writing about the extent of change, starting a point with 'By…' followed by the date can be an effective way of summarising what had been achieved over a certain period of time. Looking back over developments from the end date can be a concise way of showing that you know the key events without writing a narrative.

- Remember that you will be making judgements, so build up an appropriate vocabulary to help you express this.

Using specialist vocabulary and handling concepts sensibly

Your answers will be more convincing if you can use specialist terms appropriately. However, do not fall into the trap of using them excessively and unnecessarily – just be confident enough to use them when relevant.

Some of the mainstream terms that come up in essay titles were discussed earlier. There were also suggestions to get you started on building up your own specialist vocabulary to use in your answers.

Using the appropriate level of detail

Dates

Dates are important, as history does not make sense without them, so know the years when important things happened. At the very least you need to know the order in which events happened. Using time charts as a revision tool (see page 96) can be a really effective way of learning dates. Occasionally students go too far and think they need the actual day of the month – this is hardly ever useful.

It is important to be able to stand back from events and see them in perspective – try to get used to seeing how details fit in to the bigger picture. Too much detail obscures the broader picture, but too little leads to a hazy, unclear picture. Knowing the key dates certainly helps towards this.

Statistical evidence

Statistical evidence can be really useful, especially if you are trying to show the extent of change. However, be careful to make figures meaningful – it is not much use just saying that Russia produced 76.3 million tons of coal in 1933. However, if you then contrast this with the 35.5 million tons produced in 1928 you can make a telling comment about the rapid progress made in the First FYP and say that it nearly doubled. Round up to sensible whole numbers and remember to make clear why you have included the figures – what point are they helping you show?

Quotes

Using quotes can be a really convincing way of making a point, but always attribute them to the right person and if possible comment on the context the comment was made in. If you cannot remember the exact words, you can still say what their comment reveals. For example, if you cannot remember what Stalin allegedly said about the West in 1929 ('we are 50– 100 years behind and if we do not close the gap in 10 years they will crush us!'), it is still useful to say that Stalin expressed alarm at how far behind the West Russia had fallen economically and was worried about the possibility of being invaded if they failed to catch up quickly. However, there needs to be some reason for pointing this out – in this case you could be explaining why Russia industrialised so fast.

Quotes from historians can also add weight to your argument, but make sure they come from experts in the appropriate particular field (such as Robert Service or Sheila Fitzpatrick) not from textbooks or revision guides.

Geography

Some basic geographical knowledge is also useful in a topic like this, since the USSR was huge and contained such diverse peoples and resources. Ensure you are able to refer to other locations where important developments occurred, such as Kazakhstan, Magnitogorsk, Ukraine, Stalingrad, and so on.

Writing legibly

Examiners can only award marks for what they can read. If your writing is so poor that the examiner cannot read it, this will pull down your mark within a level because it will be seen as weak communication (see the mark scheme on pages 93–5).

Saving time in an emergency

If you find that you really are running out of time in the exam and will not be able to finish the answer in the way you had hoped to, here are two strategies to minimise the damage.

Things to do

✓ Finish your main section with a plan that shows how each paragraph would have been structured – the point, a piece of supporting factual evidence, and some words making this relevant to the wording of the question. This last piece of advice is essential because the examiner needs to see how you would be arguing the case. Many plans fail to show this because they are purely factual, so show how you would *use* a fact to make a point. A mind map may be useful provided you make it clear how your argument would develop.

✓ Write a conclusion of reasonable length and ensure it includes a supported judgement.

Tips for success

Things to do

✓ Plan your answer to focus on the question

✓ Remember PEER as you write your work

✓ Reach a clear judgement in your conclusion

Things not to do

✗ Write long slabs of description not tailored to the wording of the question.

✗ Use abbreviations instead of writing things in full. Only do this in a dire emergency if you have no time left.

✗ Learn lots of different historians' views on issues. As long as you know and understand the different ways that an event can be interpreted that will be fine – do not worry about which historian said what.

Understanding the mark scheme

The examiner puts each essay into one of five levels according to the criteria in the table on the next two pages. Your answer is then moved within the level depending on how well it meets the descriptor. Obviously, you want your answer to go into the highest possible level, so it is worth becoming familiar with the table so that you know what the examiners are looking for.

Level	Mark range	Mark scheme descriptor	What this means
1	1–6	Candidates will produce mostly simple statements. These will be supported by limited factual material, which has some accuracy and relevance, although not directed at the focus of the question. The material will be mostly generalised. There will be few, if any, links between the simple statements. **Low Level 1: 1–2 marks** The qualities of Level 1 are displayed; material is less convincing in its range and depth. **Mid-Level 1: 3–4 marks** As per descriptor. **High Level 1: 5–6 marks** The qualities of Level 1 are securely displayed; material is convincing in range and depth consistent with Level 1. The writing may have limited coherence and will be generally comprehensible, but passages will lack both clarity and organisation. The skills needed to produce effective writing will not normally be present. Frequent syntactical and/or spelling errors are likely to be present.	Answer will be made up of brief comments on the topic rather than on the question that has been set. Is likely to be generalised and inaccurate. Will be poorly written in a simple style.
2	7–12	Candidates will produce a series of simple statements supported by some accurate and relevant factual material. The analytical focus will be mostly implicit and there are likely to be only limited links between the simple statements. Material is unlikely to be developed very far. **Low Level 2: 7–8 marks** The qualities of Level 2 are displayed; material is less convincing in its range and depth. **Mid-Level 2: 9–10 marks** As per descriptor. **High Level 2: 11–12 marks** The qualities of Level 2 are securely displayed; material is convincing in range and depth consistent with Level 2. The writing will have some coherence and will be generally comprehensible, but passages will lack both clarity and organisation. Some of the skills needed to produce effective writing will be present. Frequent syntactical and/or spelling errors are likely to be present.	Answer shows some understanding of the question topic but knowledge has not been directed at the wording of the question. Material will be more accurate than at Level 1. Points raised are not explained. Again, poorly written but better organised in terms of paragraphs than at Level 1.

Level	Mark range	Mark scheme descriptor	What this means
3	13–18	Candidates' answers will attempt analysis and will show some understanding of the focus of the question. They will, however, include material which is either descriptive, and thus only implicitly relevant to the question's focus, or which strays from the focus. Factual material will be accurate but it may lack depth and/or reference to the given factor. **Low Level 3: 13–14 marks** The qualities of Level 3 are displayed; material is less convincing in its range and depth. **Mid-Level 3: 15–16 marks** As per descriptor. **High Level 3: 17–18 marks** The qualities of Level 3 are securely displayed; material is convincing in range and depth consistent with Level 3. The writing will be coherent in places but there are likely to be passages which lack clarity and/or proper organisation. Only some of the skills needed to produce convincing extended writing are likely to be present. Syntactical and/or spelling errors are likely to be present.	Answer makes some attempt to analyse the question, using mostly accurate factual material. However, it may well describe events rather than explain them, or explain them without much detail or depth. In multi-factor questions, the range of factors dealt with will be limited. It will be clearly written and have an obvious structure with paragraphs.
4	19–24	Candidates offer an analytical response which relates well to the focus of the question and which shows some understanding of the key issues contained in it. The analysis will be supported by accurate factual material which will be mostly relevant to the question asked. The selection of material may lack balance in places. **Low Level 4: 19–20 marks** The qualities of Level 4 are displayed; material is less convincing in its range and depth. **Mid-Level 4: 21–22 marks** As per descriptor. **High Level 4: 23–24 marks** The qualities of Level 4 are securely displayed; material is convincing in range and depth consistent with Level 4. The answer will show some degree of direction and control but these attributes may not be sustained throughout the answer. The candidate will demonstrate the skills needed to produce convincing extended writing but there may be passages which lack clarity or coherence. The answer is likely to include some syntactical and/or spelling errors.	It is clear that the question has been understood and the answer is directed at the wording of the question using accurate support. Some attempt has been made to reach a judgement. However, the answer may not cover all the key points or the full time span of the question and may lose focus a little occasionally. It will be very well written and clearly structured.

Level	Mark range	Mark scheme descriptor	What this means
5	25–30	Candidates offer an analytical response which directly addresses the focus of the question and which demonstrates explicit understanding of the key issues contained in it. It will be broadly balanced in its treatment of these key issues. The analysis will be supported by accurate, relevant and appropriately selected factual material which demonstrates some range and depth. **Low Level 5: 25–26 marks** The qualities of Level 5 are displayed; material is less convincing in its range and depth. **Mid-Level 5: 27–28 marks** As per descriptor. **High Level 5: 29–30 marks** The qualities of Level 5 are securely displayed; material is convincing in range and depth consistent with Level 5. The exposition will be controlled and the deployment logical. Some syntactical and/or spelling errors may be found but the writing will be coherent overall. The skills required to produce convincing extended writing will be in place.	The answer will tackle the question directly, addressing a wide range of relevant points and making links between them. As well as covering the full time period, it will show variations in the impact of different issues at different times. The relevance of points will be clearly explained and the focus on the question will be sustained. A strong concluding judgement will be reached. It will be well written and logically structured. However, even Level 5 answers are not perfect!

Preparing for the exam

Different people revise in different ways, and by now you have been doing exams for so long you may feel you have a successful revision strategy. However, History is a subject where there is a lot to learn and some new strategies might be helpful in doing this. Always try to remember why you are likely to need particular areas of knowledge – what purpose is it likely to serve? This is not a knowledge-driven exam: you should use knowledge (evidence) to support a point in your argument, not just include it because you happen to have learned it!

Time charts

You could compile a huge time chart for the whole time period 1924–53, or break it down according to the time periods covered by the four bullet points in the Specification. Adapt the column headings to suit your focus. These are good for consolidating your chronological knowledge, for making you analyse types of events and for showing links between political, socio-economic and foreign events. Here is an example of how you might start one:

Date	Political	Social/Economic	Foreign (if it influences domestic events)
1924	Death of Lenin	NEP continuing	
1927	Exile of Trotsky		
1928		Grain procurement crisis	
1929	Bukharin defeated – NEP abandoned		
1930		'Dizzy with success' – temporary halt to collectivisation	
1933		Start of Second Five-Year Plan	Hitler to power in Germany
1936	'Great Terror' began		
1938		Start of Third Five-Year Plan	
1939			Molotov–Ribbentrop Pact
1941			German invasion
1943			Victories at Stalingrad, then Kursk
1946		Fourth Five-Year Plan began	Control of E. Europe
1953	Death of Stalin		

Biographical profiles of the key individuals

Download a photo of a key figure, for example Bukharin, Kamenev, Zinoviev or Kirov. Structure a biographical portrait, as in the example below. You could use the same categories, but obviously make amendments depending on, for example, whether the subject was defending or opposing the system in power at the time. These will help you focus on individuals, and make you think about what they did and why. You could easily convert these into revision cards.

Here is an example one of Kirov. Prepare similar ones for other people.

SERGEI KIROV

Birth and background	Born 1886. Came from poor background but educated at expense of wealthy benefactors. Had become a Marxist by age of 18.
Death	Shot by lone gunman in Leningrad Party HQ, Dec. 1934, probably with connivance of NKVD – possibly on Stalin's orders
Posts held, with dates	1921–6 Communist Party manager in Azerbaijan Member of *Politburo* 1926–34 Head of Party in Leningrad (Stalin's appointee) 1934 due to be transferred to Moscow but delayed the move.
Key things he did	Stood up to Stalin – as Leningrad Party Head he reduced police harassment of dissidents. Helped to save Ryutin from death penalty 1932. Part of moderate bloc in Party hierarchy trying to slow down pace of change. Emerged at 1934 Party Congress as potential rival to Stalin after polling fewest negative votes of any candidate (Stalin included) for Party Secretary post.
Contribution to preserving/extending Communism	Had fought in Red Army in Civil War. Efficient as administrator and organiser of Party affairs. Close colleague of Stalin who supported him on most things. Skill as orator – impressive at justifying Party policies at Congress meetings. Advocate of *gulag* labour system. Leading light of next generation of leaders.
Controversies surrounding him	Extent of his liberal tendencies difficult to judge – hardliner in many respects, but did oppose some aspects of Stalin's methods. Death remains subject of numerous conspiracy theories. Death did trigger escalation of levels of Terror – first big Show Trial soon after.

Revision checklists

Prepare and fill in a revision checklist like the one below. This is only meant to be a start, but you could go through your notes and prepare a much more thorough version by adding more; or you could slim it right down to the bare essentials. Either way, it will make you analyse the content of the course in a methodical way. Only tick the *understood* column when you feel you have an aspect under control. Use the *areas of uncertainty* box to record things you need to do more work on.

Revision checklist			
People – the big names	Understood ✓	*Economic developments*	Understood ✓
Trotsky		NEP	
Kamenev		Collectivisation	
Zinoviev		Five-Year Plans	
Bukharin		Central planning	
Yezhov		Command economy	
Kirov		Grain procurement crisis	
Zhukov		Lend-lease	
Other important people		*Organisations*	
Yagoda		*Komsomol*	
Beria		NKVD	
Stakhanov		*Politburo*	
Ryutin		*Sovnarkom*	
Khrushchev		Party Congress	
		Gosplan	
		Zhenotdel	
		Orthodox Church	
Terms associated with Marxism		*Concepts and ideas*	
Proletariat		Marxism/Leninism	
Bourgeoisie		Factionalism	
Smychka		Socialism in one country	
Personality cult		Social realism	
Show Trial		Bonapartism	
Specific geographical locations		*Other terms of importance*	
Leningrad		*Gulags*	
Magnitogorsk		*Sovkhoz*	
The Ural Mountains		*Kolkhoz*	
Kazakhstan		The Great Retreat	
Stalingrad		*Yezhovshchina*	
Kursk			

(continued on the next page)

Areas of uncertainty			

Use essay planning frames

Planning frames will help you to practise how you would structure answers to previously set questions. Complete these in a disciplined way using a format such as the one below.

Question	Type of question	Key words explained	
Introduction	**Line of argument**	**Range of factors to be considered**	
Main section paragraph 1	**Point**	**Supporting evidence**	**Relevance to the case**
Main section paragraphs 2 onwards (as required) should be continued in the same format as Main section paragraph 1			
Conclusion	**Judgement**	**Main reasons for the judgement**	

And finally…

Do not memorise example answers. Read them and learn from them, but prepare for the unexpected because the same question is unlikely to crop up again. Understand and learn the topic thoroughly but answer the question in front of you, not the one you wish it had been!

Unit 1, Question 1

'Why was Stalin, and not one of his rivals, successful in the struggle for power 1924–9?' **[30 marks]**

This question requires an explanation of the reasons for Stalin's victory in the power struggle, but it is asking why it was Stalin who won as opposed to anyone else. So the focus should be on comparing the role of the key factors (posts held, personal qualities, support within the party, and so on) as they applied to Stalin and his rivals (Trotsky, Bukharin, Kamenev and Zinoviev).

Grade C student answer

The power struggle to succeed Lenin began even before his death, when he suffered a serious stroke in 1922. By 1929 Stalin had emerged victorious, having defeated Trotsky, Zinoviev, Kamenev and Bukharin. Trotsky was the obvious successor to take power but he made a series of mistakes which Stalin took advantage of and the other possible candidates for power also proved less skilful at handling situations and had certain disadvantages which went against them. Lenin's *Testament* had criticised all of them in some way so they agreed to keep it secret, otherwise the result might have been different.

Stalin was ruthless and clever at manipulating situations to his advantage. He misled Trotsky about the date of Lenin's funeral, which obviously went against him, and by forming the triumvirate along with Zinoviev and Kamenev, he isolated Trotsky and made him seem a dangerous radical who might use the Red Army to stage a military coup. Stalin's main strength was his power to control what went on inside the party. As Secretary-General he had wide powers of patronage, which meant he could control membership and promotion in the party. This meant that Stalin could pack vital Party Congress meetings with his supporters in order to get his way, for example in 1928 when he proposed dropping NEP and going instead for rapid industrialisation. Stalin was good at making alliances and then when they had served their purpose he shifted his allegiance elsewhere: he did this with the triumvirate against Trotsky and then when he worked with Bukharin.

Trotsky was expected by many to succeed Lenin because he made a big personal contribution to the coup of 1917 and to the Red victory in the Civil War. However he was arrogant and just assumed that his intellectual ☞

The introduction shows that the question has been understood and sets out the context of the struggle but fails to clearly identify the key factors that led to Stalin's victory and it shows a slight lack of focus in both the first and last comments. It implies that the outcome was due to mistakes made by the 'other contenders' combined with Stalin's opportunism but this really needs to be made clearer.

This is a stronger paragraph focusing on key strengths of Stalin, particularly his ability to undermine Trotsky and his control over party affairs. It is clearly written, the points are valid and they are supported by accurate evidence. It would be much improved however, by some comments contrasting these attributes shown by Stalin with weaknesses of the others.

ability would win any argument so he didn't bother making friends among the other leaders. This made him unpopular, as did the fact that he had been a Menshevik before 1917. He was too intellectual for many people, reading foreign novels during Politburo meetings, and it was easy for the other Bolshevik leaders to see him as a potential military dictator who might seize power using the army, and then take too many risks invading other countries to start off revolutions there as well. When Stalin, Zinoviev and Kamenev allied against him, Trotsky found himself on his own and was thrown out of the party, then out of Russia itself. No other top Bolsheviks tried to help Trotsky because he had few friends in high places so when he was in trouble he was on his own.

Zinoviev and Kamenev also had a possible chance of succeeding Lenin. Zinoviev was Party Secretary in Leningrad and Chairman of Comintern, which were both important posts. But like Trotsky, he was not personally popular with the other leaders and he had also been against the seizure of power in 1917 saying it was too soon. Kamenev had also opposed the timing of the November coup, but he was more personally popular inside the party than Zinoviev and had a Politburo post as well as being Party Chief in Moscow. The main thing that went against him was his lack of leadership qualities and his poor judgement of a situation. He showed this when he allowed himself to be manipulated by Stalin into opposing Trotsky, and then later Trotsky persuaded him and Zinoviev to form the United Opposition against Stalin and Bukharin. Both Zinoviev and Kamenev underestimated Stalin and when they asked the Congress of 1925 to pass a vote of no confidence in Stalin, it was they who got defeated and two years later they were voted out of the party.

Finally, Bukharin also had a possible chance of succeeding to power because he was generally popular, having been described by Lenin as 'the golden boy' of the party. He belonged to the younger generation of Bolsheviks and was regarded as intellectually able but not as arrogant as Trotsky. His views were more moderate and on the right wing of the party – he thought Russia needed NEP for a lot longer to get the economy gradually back on its feet. For a while he worked with Stalin, but when Stalin saw his chance to get the annual Congress to abandon NEP due to the grain crisis, Bukharin was outvoted because he didn't have supporters inside the Congress who ☞

This paragraph is packed with accurate information about Trotsky's weaknesses. While it is well written, it becomes quite descriptive and needs to be linked and contrasted to Stalin, or the other people involved, to be fully relevant to the question.

Again, this paragraph is full of accurate and pertinent material on the weaknesses of other rivals for power, Zinoviev and Kamenev, though it is clearly stronger on Kamenev. It could easily be strengthened at the end by some explanation of why Stalin was able to defeat them in 1925 because of his control of party membership and the narrower nature of their support bases.

Bukharin's weaknesses are accurately stated here, with an explanation of his final defeat implied at the end, rather than being made explicit. It would be improved by making a contrast between Stalin's flexibility and Bukharin's more rigid stance on the economy.

owed their careers to him. He had no real power base he could depend on, only general support, and so he was voted off the Politburo.

The Party Congress vote in 1928 to abandon NEP and focus on rapid industrialisation marked Stalin's victory because it had been his suggestion and those on the right of the party weren't strong enough to stop it. What made it possible for Stalin to succeed above all was the power he had built up to appoint people inside the party and pack crucial meetings with them. None of the other contenders had this type of power base to capitalise on, and they were gradually outmanoeuvred by Stalin. It also went in Stalin's favour that he took a middle line on many issues so it wasn't too hard for him to adjust his stance without seeming to contradict what he stood for. By contrast Trotsky could only ever get extreme left-wing support and Bukharin was too much on the right to widen his support base enough.

This is a useful conclusion because it provides a reminder of why 1928 can be seen as the crucial year in the struggle and then summarises the key reasons for Stalin's success, which have been referred to in the earlier paragraphs on the different contenders. The key point of party patronage has been emphasised, which indicates some evaluation is going on. However, the final point, while a valid one, would have been more effective as the basis of a separate paragraph in the essay rather than being tacked on the end here.

This student shows accurate knowledge of the weaknesses of the various contenders for power and reaches a judgement about the reasons for Stalin's victory. The answer does address the question and uses evidence from across the relevant time period of 1924–9. It is clearly constructed and well written. However, it is in the middle of level 4 because:

- it is slow to get started: there is no clear sense of direction set in the introduction
- it gets rather descriptive in places
- the paragraphs tend not to be tied back to the wording of the question, which asks why Stalin won 'and not one of his rivals'
- there needs to be more comparison and contrast between the different personalities involved, particularly with strengths possessed by Stalin but not necessarily all the others.

Many students will structure an answer like this with a paragraph on the relative merits and defects of each candidate, but there needs to be cross referencing between the contenders, which a structure focusing on reasons rather than individuals can more readily produce. If the approach based on individuals is adopted, then strong links need to be made and contrasts between the different individuals highlighted. Each paragraph will need tying up in a way that makes it explicitly relevant to the wording of the question.

Overall, this answer is **mid-level 4 and would gain 20 marks.**

Excellent Grade A student answer

Stalin's victory in the power struggle over Trotsky, Bukharin, Zinoviev and Kamenev was due to a combination of personal and practical factors. He had a ruthless and manipulative personality, with power as Party Secretary to influence decisions in his favour. He was also more skilful at exploiting situations that arose than the others, and used his moderate image to his advantage. However, he was helped by the mistakes made by his rivals and their narrower appeal.

Stalin had been Secretary-General since 1922 and used his powers to promote his supporters and sideline opponents inside the party. This was particularly effective since party membership had been allowed to double in three years under the Lenin Enrolment, and many of these new members supported Stalin either out of gratitude or as the best means of advancing their future careers. Crucial decisions regarding the direction in which Russia should go were usually taken at the annual Party Congress, and once he had been Secretary for a few years Stalin was able to pack this Congress with delegates who supported his views and therefore win crucial decisions. For example, the 1927 Congress backed Stalin's suggestion to begin a rapid drive towards industrialisation, spelling the end of NEP and signalling Stalin's break with Bukharin and the right. While the other rivals for power did hold important posts, they did not give them anything like this degree of support inside the party.

Trotsky's power came from his post as Commissar of the Red Army, with whom he was very popular. However this was a narrower power base than Stalin's and also laid Trotsky open to accusations that he might plot a military coup on the lines of Bonaparte. Once Trotsky had been removed from this position in 1925 he became isolated and no one rallied to his defence when he was expelled from the party two years later because he had no friends inside the party leadership. Both Kamenev and Zinoviev had stronger power bases than this, but they were limited to the cities of Moscow and Leningrad respectively, where they headed the party branches. Bukharin, though a Politburo member, had no party power base. Therefore, none of Stalin's rivals could control the levers of power inside the party as he could, nor could they appeal to as wide a range of supporters and this gave him a really significant advantage when crucial decisions were taken in the Annual Congress, or ☞

This is a direct introduction that establishes a focus on the question and identifies the outline of the relevant factors applying to Stalin and his rivals, which will be discussed later on. It therefore sets up the argument nicely.

The value to Stalin of his powers of patronage is clearly shown here, with precise supporting evidence including dates. However, it could be strengthened by clearer explanation of the powers that went with the post of Secretary-General. It could also be made clearer that NEP was incompatible with rapid industrialisation.

The last sentence leads neatly on to the next paragraph that provides a contrast with his rivals.

Accurate evidence about the limitations of each of Stalin's rivals in terms of their support base is supplied here and then contrasted clearly with the stronger position that Stalin's powers placed him in. Taken with the paragraph above, it makes an explicitly relevant point and shows a range of knowledge and an understanding of changing issues over time. However, the contrast with Zinoviev and Kamenev's position could be highlighted by stressing that Stalin's powers of patronage were national, while theirs were only regional. It might also have been noted that being popular on a personal level, as Bukharin was, was no substitute for having power over people's futures.

even in the Politburo which met more frequently and where Stalin as Secretary could control the agenda.

Stalin also used his image as a moderate inside the party to his advantage. Occupying the centre ground gave him the advantage of being able to win the support of those immediately to the Right and Left. It also meant he had room to change his stance on issues according to circumstances without appearing contradictory, as he did when he altered his attitude to NEP because of the grain procurement crisis in 1928. Added to this was Stalin's reputation as a non-threatening bureaucrat ('Comrade Card Index'), which made him seem a trustworthy option. By contrast, Trotsky was very much a left-wing radical, advocating world revolution and immediate industrialisation which gave him little chance of broadening his support base beyond idealistic students and army officers. Despite being in the triumvirate against Trotsky for a while, Kamenev and Zinoviev were also identified with the left wing of the party, an impression reinforced when they formed the United Opposition against Stalin and Bukharin to oppose the continuation of NEP in the mid-1920s. Meanwhile Bukharin was seen as representing the right wing of the party because of his gradual approach to change and promotion of NEP. Stalin however could put himself forward as someone safe and moderate who simply put Russia's interests first and wasn't blindly committed to any ideological stance.

Stalin was also better at exploiting Lenin's legacy than his rivals. Having encouraged Trotsky to 'miss' Lenin's funeral, by making the funeral oration himself he made sure it was he who became most closely linked to Lenin in the popular imagination. Furthermore by creating the 'Lenin cult' he made it more acceptable for Russia to be eventually run by one individual, rather than by the collective leadership which had been Lenin's preference. Stalin successfully put himself in the best position to occupy this position over the following five years by building up so much power behind the scenes and exaggerating the close links that he had maintained with Lenin.

Stalin also manipulated the ideological arguments of the time more skilfully than his rivals. Firstly, because the attempted revolutions elsewhere had failed, he argued instead for 'socialism in one country', which would involve keeping NEP and consolidating the revolution at home. This was popular with nationalists inside the party and turned opinion not only against Trotsky, ☞

There is a lot in the paragraph and, again, a wide range of precise evidence has been used to support a valid point about the strength of Stalin. The contrast with the more extreme positions of his rivals helps sustain the focus of the question on *why Stalin rather than anyone else*. It would have been even better to have pointed out that Stalin deliberately fostered this image (a sign of his political skill) while his rivals were more naïvely optimistic.

While this is a good point, which does follow on logically from the previous paragraph, it could have been even more explicitly linked to it by starting 'Further evidence of Stalin's political cunning was shown by …'. It would be even stronger if the advantage that Stalin gained from the suppression of Lenin's testament was brought in as well.

This is the first of two paragraphs illustrating how Stalin used ideological issues to discredit others – in this case on the left of the party in the earlier part of the struggle. It links to the previous point about patronage. It could be slightly improved by some comment about the way old pre-revolutionary views like nationalism remained strong and how the new revolutionary leaders were not afraid to tap in to them when there was advantage to be gained. This could be shown as another of Stalin's manipulative ploys.

who was a fanatical internationalist, but also against Zinoviev whose job as head of Comintern was to start revolutions abroad. Stalin could pack the 1925 Party Congress with his supporters, and so Zinoviev and Kamenev lost their party positions in Leningrad and Moscow.

Secondly, he discredited the preference of the right wing of the party for NEP by exploiting the grain procurement crisis of 1927–8 which was threatening urban food supplies. Thanks to the powers of patronage he enjoyed as Secretary, Stalin was able to get the Party Congress to abandon NEP in 1928 and then remove Bukharin and the other right wingers from their posts in 1929. While Stalin could not create the opportunities that these ideological arguments opened up, he was clever and ruthless enough to exploit them to his advantage.

In conclusion, Stalin emerged victorious from the power struggle because he combined skill at exploiting circumstances with wide powers of patronage so that he was confident that crucial decisions in Congress would go in his favour. He was also a skilled manipulator, setting up alliances to discredit enemies and then dropping his 'allies' when their purpose had been served. Furthermore he was able to appear moderate and trustworthy by remaining above the most vicious infighting and occupying a position in the centre, so he never became isolated in the way that his rivals did. Added to this was his preoccupation with administrative matters which had allowed him to quietly build up power behind the scenes. All these factors combined to put Stalin in a strong position from which to take full advantage of mistakes made by his rivals. In 1929 he could celebrate his fiftieth birthday as the undisputed leader of Russia.

The second example provided shows how he discredited the right and again links back to the underlying strength that party patronage gave Stalin. The evidence continues to be precisely selected and is being used to support a point. The final sentence would be even better with a contrasting comment about the inability of his main rivals to pounce when circumstances were advantageous because they lacked the support in the party to make such a move effective – and maybe the personal ruthlessness to do so anyway.

The conclusion sums up the many contributory factors dealt with earlier in the essay and reiterates the judgement already hinted at: that the powers that Stalin accrued inside the party were the most crucial to his ultimate success. Stalin's skill at manipulating people and situations comes across clearly and the final sentence provides a neat finish.

This answer tackles the question directly and sustains its focus on the wording of the question. For example, the phrase in the question 'not one of his rivals' has been addressed by frequent contrasts between the position of Stalin and other contenders and links between the main point (patronage) and the others have been frequently made. A wide range of accurate and precise supporting evidence has been used from across the full time period of 1924–9, but this evidence has been selected, not used indiscriminately.

However, the conclusion could have been strengthened by more reference to the 'not one of his rivals' part of the question: it is slightly unbalanced in that it concentrated mainly on Stalin.

This answer is clearly **Level 5 and would gain 29 marks.**

Unit 1, Question 2

'To what extent did Stalin's social and cultural policies change the lives of people in Russia in the 1930s?' [**30 marks**]

This is an extent of change question and is asking you to assess the impact of the various social and cultural policies on people. It will be more manageable to divide the population into appropriate sub-groups and to deal separately with social and cultural policies. You need to be aware that the lives of people were changed by economic and political policies as well, and it can be hard sometimes to distinguish between one type of policy and another, so pay attention to keeping the focus on social and cultural policies.

Grade C student answer

Stalin's social and cultural policies caused a great deal of change to people's lives in Russia in the 1930s because he ended the period of experimentation and started the Great Retreat which was a return to traditional approaches. The main changes applied to women, young people and the family.

Women were mainly helped by the return to traditional policies. The new Family Code brought in substantial child allowances and safeguarded marriages by making it more expensive for men to divorce their wives as soon as they got pregnant. This happened a lot in the 1920s, and women were left to bring up the children alone. Weddings were made much more glamorous occasions, with marriage certificates being printed on special paper, whereas in the 1920s people had been encouraged to see marriage as unnecessary and old fashioned and wedding rings had been banned. Women were also encouraged to get more educated under Stalin and far more females went to university and got professional careers than before. Many women also worked in the expanding factories, but they weren't allowed to play any part in political life. Most of these changes were to the advantage of women who had come off badly from the freedom of the 1920s.

Stalin wanted to promote family life because there had been a breakdown of this and it had led to thousands of orphans having to be looked after by the state and it was causing a crime wave among the young who didn't recognise any authority. Stalin feared that social breakdown like this would put the Five-Year Plans ☞

This is a short introduction that identifies relevant social groups to be examined, but gives an over-simplified impression that Stalin's policies were consistently traditional by ignoring the first few years of radical cultural revolution. It is general, in that there is no indication of the type of changes people experienced.

This paragraph provides quite a lot of accurate information about policies affecting women in the 1930s, making some valid contrasts with the 1920s. However, there is some descriptive drift regarding weddings and the fact that there was a combination of progressive and traditional policies has not been recognised. There is a final judgement, but it is rather sweeping.

This paragraph is not securely focused on the question. The factual details are valid, but the paragraph is about the reasons why Stalin wanted to restore family stability rather than being an assessment of the impact of the policy concerned.

at risk so in the Family Code men who left their wives had to make substantial maintenance contributions to the upkeep of the family, and divorces were made much harder to get. Restoring the importance of marriage helped to stabilise society and brought young people back under control.

Young people's lives were also greatly changed by the return to traditional schooling in the 1930s. In the 1920s teachers had lost the right to discipline children and formal testing and homework disappeared. Many youngsters simply stopped going to school. Stalin could see the damage this was causing to society and the economy, so he restored normal teaching methods and brought in a traditional curriculum to improve basic standards of literacy and numeracy. Apart from changing the way young people spent their time, these changes also improved young people's job prospects because levels of literacy improved enormously so more job opportunities opened up. As well as this, young people felt they were involved in building the new communist society by being in the Pioneers and then the Komsomol. These gave people a sense of purpose and helped create a sense of belonging to the future.

Stalin's cultural policies were centred on social realism, which was the only acceptable form of artistic expression allowed. This involved glorifying the working class struggle to succeed in industrialising Russia and promoting the cult of Stalin as the undisputed leader. Novels, paintings, films and music were all geared up to promoting heroic role models who ordinary people could try to copy. No one really knows how much this actually changed people's lives but it probably had more impact on younger people who had never known anything else and had been brought up as members of the Young Pioneers and then Komsomol.

In conclusion, Stalin's social and cultural policies changed people's lives a great deal because he was worried about what would happen to his economic plans if society continued to break down due to all the experimentation. Therefore he restored traditional values, which for young people meant a return to discipline and for married women it meant they got back some security in their lives. The cultural policies affected everyone because what they could read and see was controlled by the state but they didn't necessarily believe it was true or change their lives because of it. ☞

This section starts with a useful link back to the previous paragraph, but again the focus drifts briefly into why the policy changed. The rest of the paragraph is more relevant and focused on the impact on young people. However, a specific example, such as joining the Twenty-five Thousanders or informing on *kulaks,* is needed to back up the comment about sense of purpose.

This fairly concise paragraph on social realism shows that its purpose has been understood. The problem of quantifying its impact is a legitimate one to raise. A specific illustrative example of a book or film promoting these values would have strengthened it.

The conclusion starts off-focus with the explanation of why the changes came in, but then does summarise the main changes that have been dealt with earlier. It reaches a general, rather sweeping, judgement that there was indeed a great deal of change for women and young people and that the policies were traditional.

This answer does not quite reach level 4 for the following reasons:

- The focus is not quite right: although mainly focused on the question, it occasionally drifts into explaining why the policies came in when it should be focusing on the impact of these policies.
- There is some descriptive drift on marriage.
- The range of aspects is slightly limited – religious groups and social classes might have been considered.
- The depth is also a little superficial in that there is no recognition that Stalin's policies began radically and then became traditional.

However, it does have good qualities.

- It is logically constructed.
- It contains accurate evidence that is quite detailed in parts.
- There is an attempt to answer the question and to reach an overall judgement.

It could be awarded level 4 if the focus on the question were sharper and maintained.

Overall, this answer would be near the top of **level 3 and gain 18 marks**.

Grade A student answer

Stalin's social and cultural policies began in a radical way with the Cultural Revolution being launched at the same time as the First Five-Year Plan, but then became much more traditional in the so-called 'Great Retreat' from the middle of the 1930s. While Soviet propaganda claimed impressive results, announcing the existence of 'new Soviet Man' by the end of the decade, the reality was less impressive. Nevertheless, people's lives were changed significantly, particularly by the policies that targeted women, the family, young people and religion.

Stalin's policies towards women changed their lives significantly. In some respects they became more emancipated – their educational opportunities expanded to such an extent that females made up over half the population of university students by 1939, and female graduates were going into medical and engineering careers for the first time. Women were also making up over 40 per cent of the industrial workforce by the end of the decade. However, when the 'Great Retreat' began they were also expected to return to their traditional domestic roles as mothers and home-makers, so the impact of Stalin's social policies while still significant, was also contradictory and pulling women in opposite directions.

The new approach to family life which took shape in the mid '30s specifically affected married women. In general, women had been disadvantaged by the social policies of the 1920s which advocated free love, easy divorce and communal living. Most of Russia's huge number of divorces were instigated by men, escaping the responsibilities of unwanted children. However, Stalin's Family Code of 1936 brought together a package of measures, financial and legal, to strengthen marriage and restore more security particularly to married women. For example, adultery became a criminal offence and divorces and abortions more expensive, while generous family allowances were introduced and marriages were made glamorous occasions. Propaganda now stressed the need for husbands and fathers to honour their responsibilities in order to be good Soviet citizens. These were significant changes from the previous decade and restored the family to the centre of social life, giving husbands and wives incentives to stay together and forcing attitudes to marriage to change.

An important part of restoring the family was the re-imposition of parental authority over children. ☞

The introduction identifies where the focus of the answer should lie and indicates the key areas that will be examined later on. The main thrust of the argument has been made clear. The period has been put into context, which is important here as the change in the direction of many social policies makes the 1930s more complicated. The contrast between propaganda image and reality sets things up nicely.

Precise and wide-ranging evidence has been used here to support the point about the significant changes to women's lives. The complexity of the impact on women has been made clear at the end of the paragraph.

Although the paragraph focuses on family policy rather than any particular social group, accurate evidence about the changes to the lives of husbands and wives is provided. The role of propaganda underpinning the changes is referred to again and the contrast with the 1920s helps to inform the judgement of extent.

The much publicised case of Pavlik Morozov, the boy who cared more about Russia than his own family to such an extent that he 'shopped' his father as a kulak, came in the years of the Cultural Revolution: from the mid-1930s onwards, family loyalty was supposed to come first. This shift in values back towards obedience and respect was also reflected in schools where old-fashioned teaching methods, exams and homework were restored, and attendance became compulsory – unlike the earlier experiments with freedom and equality, when school attendance had dropped right off. However, as in the case of women, policies affecting young people had contradictory effects: while parental and school discipline was being restored and young people were being subjected to more control in this way, they were also being encouraged to contribute to building the new Russia through their participation in Pioneer and Komsomol activities. Furthermore, the expansion of higher education gave them access to a wider variety of career opportunities than previously, so young people were getting new opportunities while being controlled in a traditional way.

This paragraph contains a wide range of accurate evidence about changes affecting young people, at home, in education and in the youth movements. The focus on social policies causing change has been sustained. Understanding of the contradictory outcomes is clear and links with the point about women are made.

The greater emphasis on education from the mid '30s also impacted on adult workers as well as their children. There was an expansion of adult education courses to train workers for new roles in management which were opening up to them due to the purging of so-called 'bourgeois specialists'. Social mobility was increasing due to these changes which led to the creation of the 'quicksand society' where people's status could rise or fall more suddenly than in the past. This constant state of change was partly, if not entirely, created by Stalin's social policies and affected huge numbers of people, sometimes to their benefit, sometimes to their disadvantage.

This section on adult education links well to the previous one on schools and has been extended to show awareness of the greater social fluidity that developed under Stalin. The focus has been kept on the question here – where it could easily have drifted into explaining political or economic policies responsible for contributing to the 'quicksand society'.

However, Stalin's policies towards organised religion reinforced what was already happening rather than taking things in a new direction. Organised religions had been under attack since 1917 and the new law of 1929 had banned religious activities apart from in places of worship. The result of this in the 1930s was that followers continued to meet in secret and even gave financial support to their persecuted leaders. Eradicating religious belief would take a lot longer than another decade of repressive policies, so rather than destroying organised religion Stalin's policies drove it further underground. In this area therefore, Stalin's policies continued ☞

The final section on the impact of social policy is relevant and again uses accurate and precise evidence. The contrast here between the continuity in religious policy and change of the previous policies is referred to in the opening and closing sentences.

what was already changing the lives of large sections of society, rather than taking things in a new direction, so in this sense it was less of a change.

In terms of cultural policy, the new approach of social realism was supposed to inspire ordinary people to struggle against adversity in the same way as the heroic figures of the approved novels and paintings appeared to do. However, while Ostrovsky's books were the most frequently borrowed from the library in Magnitogorsk, this doesn't necessarily mean that ordinary Russians wanted to suffer the same hardships as the heroes of his novels. Although the material produced in literature, art, film and music certainly changed to conform to the new standards required, there is little evidence that the changes went beyond creating the superficial conformity required from artists, and actually changed the way ordinary Russians saw the world. Moreover, as education and literacy levels improved, a state-controlled culture and a heroic Stalin cult was likely to become less effective because people came into contact with new ideas.

In conclusion, while it is difficult to separate the impact of social policies from that of economic and political policies on people, the main groups affected by Stalin's social policies were women and young people. For both, a mixture of progressive and traditional changes were imposed on them, but their lives in 1939 were very different compared to 1930 because the formal education of young people had become a priority, the stability of the family was re-established and women were required to fulfil dual roles. The lives of many working class people also changed as they seized the chance to better themselves at the expense of middle class victims of the 'quicksand society' who lost their managerial positions – though this situation was created by a mixture of policies, not entirely social or cultural. For the devoutly religious the situation continued to be as difficult as before, so there was less obvious change. The new cultural policies, while being aimed at all Russians, will have gradually exerted less influence as improved education led people to challenge the view of life that social realism presented.

This is the only paragraph devoted to cultural policies, and provides a concise summary of the new approach and its impact, or lack of it. However, it is rather brief, which leaves the answer a little unbalanced overall.

The conclusion goes back over the key groups examined and summarises the amount of change experienced by each. Judgements on the different groups are reached rather than on society as a whole, which is valid since the picture is so varied. However, it would be strengthened by some comment about society as a whole. ☞

This is clearly a strong answer for the following reasons:

- It sustains its focus on the impact of social or cultural policies – there is no drift into impact of other policy areas.
- It deals with a wide range of social policies in some depth.
- It shows understanding of the way policies changed during the specified time period, which complicates the process of reaching a judgement.
- It reaches appropriate judgements in the conclusion, which reinforces comments made at the end of particular paragraphs.
- It follows a clear and logical structure, making some appropriate links between paragraphs.
- It is clearly expressed throughout.

However, it is a little unbalanced in terms of the treatment of cultural policies. These are summarised concisely but the answer would have been strengthened by including one less social point and expanding the cultural section to look at one particular aspect in more detail. The conclusion needs to include overall judgement about the extent of change as well as the comments specific to different groups.

Overall, this answer would achieve a secure **level 5 and 27 marks**.

Unit 1, Question 3

'How far do you agree that the most important consequence of the Five-Year Plans was that they strengthened Stalin's control over Russia?' [**30 marks**]

This question is asking you to assess the consequences of the Five-Year Plans, and reach a judgement over whether the consequence suggested in the question was the most important by contrasting it with other consequences. You need to identify these in the introduction, and then in the main part connect them with the Five-Year Plans, explain why they were important and reach a judgement about the extent of their importance. You will need to be clear in your mind how you intend to judge importance: how long the impact lasted and how many people it affected would be logical criteria to use. Break down the consequences into political (stated factor), economic and social to make your assessment manageable.

Grade C student answer

The Five-Year Plans had a range of important consequences, which included further strengthening Stalin's control of Russia soon after he had won the power struggle of the 1920s. They also led to Russia being transformed economically into a modern industrialised power which was capable of defeating the German invasion in World War Two, and caused great social upheavals in people's lives.

> The introduction identifies three relevant consequences – the stated one and two others – but gives no indication of which of these consequences was the most important. There is brief but useful context.

Stalin finally won the power struggle in 1928 when he persuaded the party to begin the Five-Year Plans to industrialise the country as quickly as possible and abandon NEP which was only changing the economy slowly. By doing this Stalin defeated his rivals on the right of the party who wanted to keep NEP, so in a sense it was the actual decision to start the Five-Year Plans that was vital to Stalin's control. However, the continued success of the plans in boosting output of heavy industrial goods added to Stalin's control and he was able to silence critics like Kirov who said the changes were coming too fast. Russia tripled its output of coal and steel and rearmed enough to deal with the Germans when they eventually attacked in 1941. Stalin had said at his 50th birthday party that 'we are 50 years behind the west and if we don't catch up in 10 years they will crush us' and events seemed to prove him right. This therefore greatly strengthened his control over the Communist Party and over Russia. ☞

> The paragraph deals with the stated consequence and shows two ways in which the Five-Year Plans did strengthen Stalin's control. The factual support is accurate and the final comment directly addresses the question.

However, another important consequence of the Five-Year Plans was that they changed the economy of Russia out of all recognition. Russia went from being a traditional agricultural country to being a modern industrial power with huge cities and a large industrial working class working in factories. Farms needed less workers because of collectivisation and this released thousands of peasants to move to the cities where they became industrial workers. Under the plans, high targets were set and strictly enforced which led to impressively high output levels of heavy industrial goods, even if managers falsified statistics to protect themselves and the quality was often poor. Some huge new projects like the Magnitogorsk steel works were put into operation. Modernisation like this would not have happened without the target setting and discipline of the Plans and the Russian economy was rapidly modernised as a result. If NEP had continued, industry would not have grown in this way at all because it was designed to settle production down after the Civil War, not to rush the country forwards in preparing for a war against foreign enemies, and it involved no planning by the state.

> This section is devoted to explaining the main economic consequences of the Plans and uses accurate evidence to do this. The contrast with NEP is useful in highlighting the different outcomes, but it could easily be strengthened by a little more explanation of the role of centralised planning in forcing change.

These changes to the economy also had dramatic consequences for the Russian workers whose lives were turned upside down by the Plans. Peasants became industrial workers and had to adapt to a different way of working and terrible living conditions in the rapidly growing cities. Many were labelled as kulaks and they ended up as slave labourers in the gulags. Working hours were much longer and they did a seven day week with hardly any consumer goods to buy with their wages. Also, many families were permanently broken up by the change to collective farms, so the social upheavals involved were also very significant, particularly for the peasants who had got used to farming their private plots of land and selling their surplus to make a profit. The Five-Year Plans put an end to the difference between the towns and the countryside and everyone was now treated technically the same.

> This paragraph on the social impact of the Five-Year Plans contains quite a bit of descriptive material but it is reasonably concise and is relevant to the plans. However, it could have been presented more analytically by linking the consequences clearly to the centralised nature of the Plans – 'because everything was planned centrally by Gosplan, peasants'. While the final comment is valid, it does not add anything to the paragraph.

Overall, the most important consequence of the Five-Year Plans was the way they changed the economy into a modern industrial one because this enabled Russia to prepare for the Nazi invasion and eventually drive the Germans out. Not only had the Russians developed the capacity to produce what they needed to fight in terms of weapons and industrial goods, but the plans got the people used to strict discipline and shortages so they ☞

> The conclusion does clarify the line of argument and a judgement has been reached that is consistent with what has been written in the main part of the answer.

were able to keep going despite the desperate conditions of the war. The strengthening of Stalin's power was also an important consequence but not so important because he had already won the power struggle and was becoming a dictator in any case – the Plans helped him increase what he already had. The social changes were dramatic but not so important because ever since 1917 the lives of the Russian people had been constantly changing.

The student has clearly understood the question and directed the answer towards it.

- Supporting evidence is generally accurate.
- The range covers the relevant key areas.
- Depth of explanation is adequate and points are made relevant to the question.
- It is structured in a clear and logical way and written coherently.

However, there are areas where the focus drifts slightly, for example where the economic consequences are described, and at the end of the paragraph on social consequences. The introduction failed to indicate which type of consequence was most important and did not explicitly establish criteria for judging importance. The range of consequences, while adequate, could be extended further by more careful examination of the political consequences that impacted on Stalin.

Overall, this answer would achieve mid **level 4 and 20 marks**.

Grade A student answer

The strengthening of Stalin's control over Russia that the Five-Year Plans undoubtedly produced had a very significant impact because it helped secure Stalin's position and enabled him to continue as dictator until his death in 1953. However, more important than strengthening Stalin's personal control, the Five-Year Plans also transformed the Russian economy from that of a backward agricultural society into a modern industrialised state that proved capable of resisting German invasion and then controlling much of Eastern Europe after 1945. Although these two consequences are connected, the economic transformation of Russia was more significant because it lasted such a long time. The Plans also had profound effects on Russian society as a whole, as well as on the thousands of individuals whose lives were turned upside down by them.

Stalin's control over Russia was strengthened by the Five-Year Plans because they marked a clear break from Lenin's Russia which had been based on a temporary compromise with capitalism through the adoption of NEP. By getting the party to agree to rapid industrialisation in 1928, and carrying it through despite the protests of moderates who thought the first plan had gone too fast, Stalin was able to impose his personal stamp on Russia. *Pravda* now depicted him as a new leader on a par with Lenin who was taking Russia forward to the next stage of revolution, and ending the distasteful compromise with capitalism that NEP had necessitated in the 1920s. The successful pushing through of the Plans provided plenty of propaganda material to reinforce the impression that it was Stalin who now decided Russia's future – he wasn't merely following in Lenin's footsteps.

Stalin's control over the Russian workers was also strengthened by the way the Five-Year Plans worked. Centralised control and top down management, with strict discipline and relentless pressure on everyone to meet targets or face the consequences, put Stalin as party leader in a dominant position. While there was significant grass roots support for the Five-Year Plans from urban workers and the younger generation, the system was built to operate from the top downwards, and there was no doubt that Stalin stood at the top. Much later, when the Germans did invade in 1941, the fears that Stalin had voiced back in 1929 about modernising in 10 years or 'the West will crush us' seemed justified and added to Stalin's reputation as the forward-looking leader who knew what was best for Russia. Therefore in political terms, a key outcome of   ☞

The introduction identifies three important consequences and indicates the line of argument the answer will take – that the economic transformation of Russia was an even more important consequence than the stated consequence. It implies the criteria that will be used to judge importance, but would be even better if it made these explicit as suggested in the first piece of commentary above.

The first main paragraph makes a clear point in support of the stated consequence. It links the Five-Year Plans to the growth in Stalin's power by making the contrast with Lenin, and uses accurate contextual knowledge.

This makes a second point about the stated consequence. It could be made clearer that the chain of command started with Stalin and that subordinates felt compelled to 'work towards' him. The stated consequence has been nicely summed up in the final sentence.

the Plans was to greatly strengthen Stalin's control and allow him to be depicted in *Pravda* as the great *vozhd* who had masterminded this achievement.

A further political consequence of the Plans, but not one related directly to Stalin's power, was that they ensured that Russia would continue to develop along communist lines and break away from capitalism. Although elements of capitalism reappeared in the form of incentives once the Stakhanovite movement got established, the break with capitalism had really been made when NEP was abandoned and the propaganda could boast of full employment and high productivity in communist Russia while the capitalist West remained in depression. The Five-Year Plans committed Russia to a communist future and made sure that what had already been achieved was not going to be lost because of compromise. This was a truly significant outcome since it laid the basis for the next 50 years, not only of Russia, but also of Eastern Europe when the USSR took over after 1945.

The answer is continuing to sustain its focus on the question and here a further relevant point is being made about the political consequences of the plans. With a reference to Stalin's own ideology it could be made directly part of the stated consequence, but it stands up in any case as another important outcome of the Plans and shows a clear perspective of the period.

However, in economic terms, the Five-Year Plans had the even more significant consequence of transforming Russia from a peasant to an industrial economy in a very short span of time – it is often said that Russia went from the wooden plough to the nuclear reactor in a single generation, which is clearly a tremendous change, and one which could not have happened so quickly without the Plans. Even if quality of goods was often poor, by setting, and constantly raising, production targets for everything and enforcing discipline through a culture of fear, Gosplan forced Russia's output up rapidly and the heavy industrial base for rearmament was successfully put in place. For example, coal production increased by 40 million tonnes from 1928 to 1933 and electricity generation increased seven fold in the 1930s. While Russia's ability to resist German invasion after 1941 was also due to other factors, it would not have been possible at all without these economic developments in the 1930s. The role of central planning in all this was crucial which is why such changes could not have happened so fast under NEP.

This is an effective start to the paragraph since it is made explicitly clear that the argument is now moving from political to economic consequences. It is based on a strong point about the speed of change and the importance of rearmament. The factual support is accurate and contextual understanding is clear from the comments about targets. However, it would be further improved if it were made explicitly clear why such changes would not have been possible under NEP. It really needs a stronger finishing comment to underline that the consequences were therefore not limited to increasing Stalin's power.

Finally, the Five-Year Plans also exerted a significant influence on Russian society since so many people's lives were changed for ever by them. Since the expansion of industry required far more workers, the urban population doubled as former peasants poured in to the cities, along with kulaks from the gulags who were used as slave labourers. Also, far more women entered the workforce and higher education became available ☞

This deals with the final main consequence of the argument, the social impact of the Plans, referring to a range of social changes. Like the previous paragraph, a final comment comparing these consequences with the political ones (the stated consequence of the question) would focus the argument more sharply.

to more people. In terms of psychological impact, it may not have created 'Homo Sovieticus', the new citizen whose mindset was totally conditioned to keeping the revolution going, but the experience of living during the Five-Year Plans did have a significant impact on millions of people's lives so did have huge social consequences.

In conclusion, while the apparent success of the Five-Year Plans did certainly help to strengthen Stalin's control of Russia by ensuring that no challenges to his leadership stood any chance of gathering support, as far as Russia as a whole was concerned the most important consequences were the economic changes that transformed the country so rapidly and for so long. The Plans committed Russia to a future based on communism, rather than a mixed economy with capitalist elements, and helped Russia resist German invasion in 1941. However, this economic success also increased Stalin's control over Russia, so the consequences are closely connected. In the course of carrying through the Plans, Russian society also underwent drastic changes, although it is impossible to work out how deep these really went since people had to adapt purely in order to survive, which makes it harder to weigh up the social consequences.

The conclusion does sum up the way the argument has been put, and restates the strong links that exist between the two main strands of consequences (political and economic) that have been explained. The third element of social impact is very valid, but less well integrated into the argument. If the criteria for judging importance had been made clearer, then the difficulty of weighing up the social consequences would have been more straightforward.

Clearly the answer does address the question head on and sustains a focused approach to assessing the consequences of the Five-Year Plans.

- Links are made between the various consequences.
- It refers to long- and short-term outcomes, including some post-1945 references. There are no dates in the question, so the answer can include material up to 1953.
- It reaches a clear overall judgement in line with the way the case has been argued in the main part of the answer.
- It shows good contextual knowledge of the period, covering political, economic and social issues in appropriate depth with hints of cultural issues.
- It is well written with strong communication skills.

However, it stays at the bottom of the level because the criteria for judging importance have been left rather implicit. There are references to long-term impact and numbers but these are not directly referred to and doing so would have strengthened the answer significantly because it would have been clearer what the judgement was being based on.

Also, the sections on the 'additional' consequences could have been finished much more strongly by comparing their significance with the stated political one of the question. Again this would have made it more obvious why the final judgement had been reached.

Overall, this answer would achieve **level 5 and 28 marks**.

Unit 1, Question 4

'How accurate is it to say that Stalin's leadership was the main reason why the USSR was able to defeat Germany by 1945?' **[30 marks]**

This is a causation question where you have to weigh up the importance of a given factor (Stalin's leadership) against the importance of other factors in accounting for the USSR's victory over Germany. Although the time period of the war was 1941–5, you will need to consider some actions taken before 1941 in explaining the end result. You need to reach a clear judgement about the relative importance of the factors and specifically of Stalin's leadership.

Grade C student answer

The leadership shown by Stalin was one of the reasons why Russia won the war against Germany but there were others such as the mistakes made by the Germans, the determination of the Russian people, the economic situation in Russia and the help they got from the allies. It seems that Russia's success was due to a mixture of all these factors.

This addresses the question and identifies a range of valid reasons to be examined later on. It is a simple but effective start.

Stalin had been giving strong leadership to Russia for over ten years when the war broke out so it was no surprise that he continued in the same way during the war. One of the main things he did was to ban the government from fleeing from Moscow, so they were risking their lives in the same way as the population in general. Russian propaganda always stressed Stalin's role as the father of the nation, so staying to face the Germans in Moscow helped consolidate this impression. Stalin also took the decision to call off the persecution of the Orthodox Church, which helped win the support of the Christians and boosted their morale.

This paragraph considers two aspects of Stalin's leadership that helped Russia. It is accurate but would be better if each of the two aspects had been explained more fully, for example to explain that the more relaxed religious policy is relevant because it meant the Church threw its weight behind the war in return, which encouraged people to fight harder.

One main reason for the Russian victory was the many mistakes made by the Germans. Firstly, Hitler was over-confident and interfered with decisions he should have left to his generals, but he was no military strategist so this caused problems. Secondly, the German army was under-equipped for the harsh Russian winter and Hitler delayed the attack until late June 1941, which was too late in the year. Thirdly, he attacked too many targets at once, which over-stretched the armies and made supplying them more difficult. Putting the Russian cities under siege was a tactic that took time and allowed the Russians to regroup. ☞

This paragraph contains accurate details of German errors. It would benefit from some linkage with the previous point and from examples of the different errors, for example of a 'problem' arising from Hitler's interference, a city under siege, and so on.

Leningrad survived under siege for 900 days, which shows the incredible resistance of the Russians and was another reason for their victory. The Russians fought harder because of the brutality the Nazis showed as they advanced and Stalin was quick to announce that this was a war to defend the 'Motherland', not a war to defend the idea of communism which motivated people to fight on.

This point links well with the previous one and identifies a further valid reason for Russia's victory, but is poorly developed. There are other aspects of the point that might have been explained: how Nazi racism against Slavs backfired on them, why the Germans might have been seen as 'liberators' initially, and so on. The point could be linked to Stalin's leadership skill (seizing the chance to appeal to nationalism because he knew his own policies had lost him goodwill) and to the point in the middle of the following paragraph about the workers being hardened for conflict.

In addition, Russia emerged victorious because of the way the economy had improved in the 1930s and really focused on rearmament in the Third Five-Year Plan. The Russians were producing more tanks than the Germans, and because of the Russian scorched earth retreat policy it was impossible for the Germans to pick up supplies locally. The Russian workers were already used to rationing before the war so had no problem adapting to the hardships of wartime. Also the Russians made their women work in factories, but in Germany they were treated more carefully.

There is a lot of valid and accurate information about the Russian economy here but it becomes fragmented as the answer moves on to a new point before the relevance of the previous one has been clearly explained. Each element needs properly explaining. For example, it would have been useful to comment on the huge distances that the German supply lines had to stretch and the destruction of the rail system by the retreating Russians in order to fully explain the point about scorched earth restricting the Germans.

Another reason for Russia's victory was the economic aid they got from being in the Grand Alliance with the USA and GB. Because of this Russia had access to help through the lend-lease scheme which was vital in terms of food and transport. They got nearly 2000 railway engines from the USA and tinned Spam supplied the soldiers with food which was vital for keeping the Red army supplied because the Russian economy was focused on producing arms not consumer goods. Another benefit from being in this alliance was that the British were bombing German factories so it was even harder for the Germans to keep their armies supplied.

The final point is made much more fully and using precise supporting detail. Obtaining these benefits from the alliance could have been linked back to Stalin's leadership by referring to his skill in accessing foreign aid despite the antagonism of the West towards communism, and the meetings he had with Western leaders. Note that the abbreviation 'USA' is acceptable; however, the canditdate should have written Britain rather than 'GB' for clarity.

In conclusion, Stalin's leadership was an important factor in Russia's victory, but in the end it was due to the combination of all of them: the military mistakes made by the Germans stopped them from conquering Russia in the first year and then the economic preparations that had gone on in the Five-Year Plans proved their worth. However, if the Russian people hadn't been so determined to keep on struggling the Germans would have won anyway, so it was due to a combination of all these reasons that Russia drove the Germans back from 1943 onwards. ☞

The final paragraph attempts to draw the factors together by showing the inter-relationship between four of them, reaching the conclusion that Russia's victory cannot be attributed to any single factor, but a combination that includes Stalin's leadership among others. Although it sits on the fence, the judgement is valid because it is supported by the evidence examined earlier.

It is clear that the student has understood the question and the answer is directed at it throughout. There is no problem with the focus and each paragraph makes a valid point. The supporting evidence is accurate and it is clearly argued.

However, depth is lacking in many places (with the notable exception of the lend-lease point) and there is little detailed support provided. The relevance of points is often left implicit rather than being stressed at the end of a paragraph, such as in the first main point on Stalin's leadership and the value of easing off on the Orthodox Church.

Mostly, the paragraphs have not been linked together very effectively, resulting in a fragmented answer (with the exception of the two linked points about the sieges in paragraphs three and four).

Overall, this answer would achieve **level 4 and 20 marks**.

Grade A student answer

Stalin's leadership was one of many important reasons that account for the USSR defeating Germany by 1945, the other main contributory reasons being the economic power of the USSR, the sheer hard work of the population, the economic aid supplied by Russia's allies and military miscalculations by the Germans. In the end, it was a combination of all these reasons that enabled the Russians to defeat the Germans, not any single reason on its own.

This is a direct and uncomplicated introduction, identifying a range of key factors and indicating how the answer will be argued.

Although Stalin's overall leadership certainly was an important factor in accounting for Russia's victory, his initial reluctance to accept the reality of the situation was the very opposite of commanding leadership. Nevertheless, once he had recovered his nerve and realised that the other Communist leaders weren't going to overthrow him, he asserted himself decisively and by declaring to the nation that Russia was involved in the 'Great Patriotic War' he took the first of several key pragmatic decisions that eventually helped Russia to win. Stalin realised that people, especially peasants who had suffered from collectivisation, would fight harder for their country than for any ideology, so stressing nationalism and suspicion of the West was a clever move. It was a call which motivated ordinary Russians more readily than an appeal to save communism would have done. A second pragmatic decision from Stalin was to ease off the persecution of the Orthodox Church in 1943. By allowing the re-opening of churches and letting the Church elect a Patriarch for the first time since 1917, the morale of the Christian population was boosted and Stalin got the backing of the clergy who preached that it was a 'holy' war against the Germans. Both these decisions showed Stalin's skill at adjusting his ideology to get short-term gains and both helped boost public morale.

The paragraph supplies precise evidence to show two examples of pragmatic decision-making that are used to demonstrate Stalin's leadership skills. The focus has immediately settled on the question. The relevance of the point has been emphasised in the final comment.

Another decision which improved civilian morale was Stalin's insistence that the leadership remain in Moscow when it seemed about to fall at the end of 1941, rather than retreat east to somewhere safer. This was a further example of his positive leadership which set an inspiring example to the population in general and helped stiffen the resolve of the people of Leningrad and Stalingrad when they endured the long sieges of their cities. The capacity of these two besieged cities to hold out so long weakened German resolve and can be at least partly attributed to Stalin's leadership because he was insisting the party leadership in Moscow put their lives at risk in the same way as everyone else. ☞

A third positive decision taken by Stalin is explained, and linked to the previous two. Linking Stalin's leadership to the weakening of the German campaign is also a strength of the paragraph, which could be improved further by elaborating on the difficulties caused to the Germans by being tied down in such exhausting sieges.

However, Stalin also made plenty of mistakes, especially in 1941 when he discounted intelligence that the invasion was about to start and then when he refused to let Zhukov retreat from Kiev, causing enormous Russian losses, so although certain aspects of his leadership contributed significantly to Russia's victory, there were more significant reasons as well and Russia's victory can't be attributed to his leadership alone.

This is a useful short paragraph because it puts Stalin's leadership in better perspective by illustrating two precise negative examples and because it draws the stated factor section to an end and sets up the discussion of the role of wider factors in the next few paragraphs. The answer is following a clear and logical structure.

The sheer economic might of Russia, which was being directed towards war throughout the 1930s, and especially during the Third Five-Year Plan, was fundamental to their success. Not only had Russia had been rearming for years, she had also been relocating key industries to the east where they would be able to carry on producing out of reach of Western invaders. Despite all the losses to the Germans in 1941–2, by 1943 Russia was outproducing them in weapons, tanks and planes which meant they could outgun the Germans in most battles once the enemy advance had ground to a halt. This was only possible for two reasons: one organisational, the other human. In organisational terms, the economy had been put under central control at the start of the Five-Year Plans, so control of the economy in wartime was an easy transition and it enables military goods to be prioritised. Secondly, without the extraordinary human effort made by the workforce none of this would have mattered. However, ordinary Russians, motivated by a combination of nationalism, fear and innate toughness, worked a seven day week on long shifts for the duration of the war. They were already used to going without consumer goods and large numbers of women were already working in industry, making it easy for them to adapt and harness their economic potential to the war effort effectively. This was therefore absolutely vital to their eventual success.

This is a really well supported paragraph on what is being seen as the main reason for Russia's victory. The factual support is wide-ranging and precise, and used to show why the factor counted for so much. An appropriate focus is being sustained, and the final comment again brings it back to the question.

While the Russians did produce most of their own military goods, they did also benefit from allied economic aid which became available under the lend-lease agreement. American-made trucks and railway engines enabled the Red Army to be supplied over long distances and vast quantities of Spam provided much of the soldiers' calorie intake. This may not have been as important as the economic production of the Russians themselves, since they could produce the bulk of their own arms requirements, but it did lead Khrushchev to comment later that the Red Army could not have survived without it. ☞

This point is linked nicely to the main economic factor and the importance is made clear by Khrushchev's comment about Spam. The secondary importance of this as a factor is clear from the start of the second sentence, where the importance of the factor is being evaluated, as level 5 requires.

Finally, Russia's victory also owed a certain amount to military mistakes made by the invading Germans. Launching the attack at the end of June 1941 was optimistic as it left only a few weeks of summer to campaign, as was the decision to split their attack into three prongs rather than concentrating on taking Moscow, where the Russian government could have been overthrown. Hitler made things worse by interfering with military decisions, most famously during the battle for Stalingrad where retreat was forbidden, leading to the capture of the entire Sixth Army. Welcomed as liberators at first, the Germans threw away this advantage by their racist attitudes and savage treatment of the Russians, a situation that Stalin was quick to exploit with his call to defend the 'Motherland' from the barbaric invaders.

This is the last of the 'additional' factors discussed, and again relevant evidence is provided to support the point about German mistakes. However, several elements of the paragraph could be explained more fully, for example the inclusion of more dates to show how little time the Germans left themselves; a clearer explanation of the difficulties created by splitting the invasion force. A final comment to sum up its importance would add weight to the point.

In conclusion, Stalin's wartime leadership certainly made a significant contribution to Russia's victory. He created an image of himself as sharing the dangers of war by remaining in Moscow at the most dangerous moment and made clever tactical adjustments in his ideology to boost public morale. However, Russia's eventual victory was due to a combination of factors, of which the most important was the ability of the Russians to utilise their economic potential. This was only possible because of the Five-Year Plans that had been going on since 1928, and because of the extraordinary human efforts of the Russian people to keep going against the odds before the tide turned after the relief of Stalingrad in early 1943.

The conclusion sums up the relative importance of the points that have been discussed, and reaches an overall judgement that is in line with how the answer was written.

In this answer the student focuses on the question throughout.

- There is no drift away into another angle of the topic or into narrative of events.
- A reasonably wide range of factors has been examined, and the evidence presented is accurate and precise.
- The relevance of each point has been explicitly made, usually at the end of the paragraph.
- The structure is clear and logical, with the transition from one point to the next being easy to follow.
- It is coherently written and shows a confidence with specialist terms as appropriate.

However, it is not at the top of the level because in some paragraphs, notably on German mistakes, the explanations are not fully developed. In addition, it is somewhat unbalanced because the emphasis is largely on what the Russians did well, rather than on what the Germans got wrong.

Overall, this answer would achieve **level 5 and 28 marks.**